HOW TO APOLOGIZE TO YOUR WOMAN

...so that she won't
use it against you in the future

Karen Field Bolek

Bolekian Perspective Publishing

How to Apologize to Your Woman…so that she won't use it against you in the future.

© 2011 Karen Field Bolek.

Book cover by Ellie Searl.
Head shot photography by Tina Smothers.

Published April 2011 by Bolekian Perspective Publishing.
Written and published in the United States of America.

Library of Congress copyright application filed 2-16-2011.
ISBN 978-0-9833646-0-3

This book is dedicated to men who want to become more effective leaders in their relationships with women.

Table of Contents

Why I Wrote This Book, and Who Helped

Apologizing is among the most difficult but interesting topics I have come to understand through the course of living, both because of my own shortcomings in apologizing and because of apologies received or not received. Yet after I considered writing a book about how to apologize (at my husband's suggestion), I learned that many good books on the topic already exist (see p. 212). Realizing I had little insight into some types of apologies, including man-to-man and woman-to-man apologies, I decided to focus on what I know from experience: how a man can apologize effectively to the woman he loves. It's not that I believe men should apologize to women more often than women should apologize to men. It's just that it's easier to know if an apology is effective when you're on the receiving end of it than when you're delivering it.

Ultimately, I wanted to provide useful information on the connection between leadership and effective apologies, especially as it pertains to men as leaders in their personal relationships with women. For any reader who feels devalued by my topic, whether it's because you don't like to be told what to do or because you're not heterosexual, not a man, not in a relationship, or for any other reason, let me say that I mean no disrespect. My intention is simply to write about a particular area of apologizing that I feel I understand, not to boss, blame, or marginalize anyone. Some of the ideas expressed in this book may easily apply to people in other types of relationships, and I hope that everyone can find value in the basic messages of the book, including the mechanics of apologizing effectively, the skill of fictional listening, and the link between apologizing and good leadership.

To those men and women who helped me develop the book's basic concepts, I am most grateful. First and foremost, my husband, Jim Bolek, has given me a reason to care about the topic and has listened with passion, intellectual interest, and manly courage to my thoughts about it. Second, my friend Lee S. Johnsen of Partners in Development partnered with me for more than two years out of friendship and an interest in communication skills as he helped me develop my Focus Triangle learning model, providing me with just the right combination of questions, encouragement, and challenges. Simultaneously, my friend and cousin basia of Amethyst Gallery helped to bring the Focus Triangle to life, absorbing its importance during our conversations and encouraging its further development. In addition, I appreciate the countless people throughout my life who have displayed examples of effective and ineffective apologies in everyday situations, enabling me to analyze differences among them.

To my editors, Jim, Alicia, Andrea, and Lee: thank you very much for your time and effort, suggestions and guidance. First-draft editors Jim Bolek and my friend Alicia Dale of Full Circle Management contributed edits that were often gender-relevant and comments that helped me rethink and reshape the text. Later, my friend Andrea Burleson-Rutter, Ph.D., an organizational psychologist, provided a thorough edit as well as guidance in developing the Men's Apology Survey. Finally, Jim Bolek and Lee Johnsen supplied final edits.

Professional contributors I want to thank include graphic design expert Ellie Searl for her cover and publishing logo design; intellectual property attorney Daliah Saper for her legal counsel; Tina Smothers for her headshot photography; and business coach Jim Kelly of Real Leaders Lead for his wise counsel. Thanks also to the professionals at CreateSpace and Amazon.com for their book production and distribution services.

As for survey contributors, I owe many thanks to the 170 anonymous survey participants who took time to complete the Men's Apology Survey. Thanks also to my friends Terri Calvert and Heather Crockett for their survey recruiting efforts; to Craigslist for enabling me to recruit participants in remote locations; to all my friends in Toastmasters District 30, the Midwest Writers Association, Author! Author!, and the Lake Forest College Master of Liberal Studies program who lent their support; and to the inimitable Lennie Rose and the Big Ooga network for helping me cross the finish line. Thanks as well to Survey Monkey for making it possible to conduct my Men's Apology Survey online.

Finally, I want to thank all the friends, relatives, and educators who encouraged me over the years to develop my thinking and writing. Special thanks to Professors Carol Gayle and Dan LeMahieu of the graduate program at Lake Forest College for recognizing my brand of intelligence, helping me develop it, and remaining interested in my success.

Friends have offered business skills and new business associates have become friends. It's been a rewarding journey.

~ Karen Field Bolek

1

WHY APOLOGIZE?

It's not hard to understand why many men don't apologize as often as women would like. Topping the list are the risk of failure and the rejection and abuse that failure can bring. Possible loss of power in the relationship is another major concern. Thoughts of shame, embarrassment, or humiliation, and a dread of the sinking sense of incompetence loom large in the imagination. Even those with the best of intentions report being wary of possibly "opening up a can of worms" by apologizing. On the other hand, not apologizing at all can sometimes get a man into at least as much trouble as can apologizing ineffectively.

Avoiding an apology makes some sense if you don't have a clear concept of how to pull it off and gain closure while maintaining your dignity in the process. Conversely, if you were given a practical, systematic technique for apologizing effectively when appropriate – one that would enable you to look strong and even gain stature in the relationship – you might be more inclined to try it and ultimately to apologize a little more often.

This book is not designed to convince you that you *should* apologize in every case. Rather, it shows you how to apologize effectively when you *choose* to do so and how apologizing effectively when appropriate will benefit and empower you in your relationship with your woman. As you'll see, apologizing effectively is a gateway skill to becoming a better leader. And in the close personal realm, becoming a better leader translates to becoming the man your woman will admire more, have a greater desire to please, and be more eager to follow.

Before discussing types of leadership and how apologizing effectively will help you develop your leadership skills, let's take a look at male–female relationships from the male perspective.

THE RIDDLE OF MANHOOD

Manhood itself contains a riddle: as a man you need a partner, and yet you also need to feel strong and self-sufficient. How can you be both independent and attached?

When you're in a close personal relationship with a woman, it's sometimes hard to feel strong and self-sufficient because being around her makes you feel how much you need her. At times you may try to discount her importance to convince yourself that you're strong and independent and don't *really* need her. Then, when she sometimes gets upset at being discounted, and especially when she gets mad at you for something specific that you do or say that seems to discount her importance, it's even harder to feel strong and self-sufficient because you don't always know what to do to make her feel better, or to make her stop complaining and be nice to you again. This riddle of manhood may sometimes appear to be a plot devised by women to defeat you in the battle of the sexes, rather than a situation into which you were born, a part of your male human condition.

The key to solving this riddle, and to becoming stronger and more self-sufficient even in the midst of a long-term love relationship, is embedded in the practices of what I call "strong positive leadership," or what business expert Stephen R. Covey, author of *The 7 Habits of Highly Effective People*, calls "principle-centered leadership."[1] Said differently, the way to square the circle of being a man, strongly independent and yet in need of a close personal relationship, is to gain power in the relationship by applying many of the leadership skills promoted as best practices in the business world.

A successful business leader uses win-win strategies in activities and negotiations. When a leader acts as a positive role model, develops people, and motivates them to be productive, his actions benefit the subordinates, the company, and himself as a leader. Similarly, a man who functions as a strong positive leader with his woman sets up win-win situations with her whenever possible. In relationship activities and negotiations, he finds opportunities to elevate his leadership stature by looking for ways to encourage and motivate her to grow and flourish, earning her loyalty in return. He also acts as a role model by showing her how to acknowledge mistakes and apologize for them appropriately, so that when it's her turn to apologize, she can follow his lead.

Equality

In western society, leadership in a love relationship is more complicated today than it was in the past. Years ago, a man could call the shots in his family and feel he was justified in doing and saying whatever he felt was right, regardless of how his woman felt about it. Historical evidence of this male attitude abounds in television programs and films. For instance, although it's debatable whether the 1957 film *Gunfight at the O.K. Corral* reflects the way men treated women in the Wild West or the way men in 1957 thought about women, this movie clearly depicts American men's degrading attitudes toward women. In many countries, men still make major decisions affecting their women without giving their women an equal voice – or any voice at all. But most women in the western world today demand equality. They exert their power by voicing their desires and opinions, becoming educated, and often working outside the home or being active in social organizations. As a result, western women have increased leverage in their primary relationships.

To have a successful relationship in western society today, most men aspire to be equals as well as leaders. This means leading part of the time, letting her lead at other times, and co-leading or negotiating sometimes so that, on the whole, you both feel powerful in the relationship. As Covey explains, being principle centered in terms of your relationship means perceiving your spouse as an "equal partner in a mutually beneficial interdependent relationship."[2]

Being interdependent and treating your woman as an equal doesn't mean you *are* equal in all ways. She can't do a lot of the things you can, and vice versa. When she makes a mistake, it's not equally your fault, just as when you make a mistake, it's not equally her fault. Nor should you have to be co-leaders and be agreeable in every decision just to be equals. In some situations you're more fit to lead. In others, she's more fit to lead. That's part of the idea of interdependence.

Leadership Challenges

Whenever you agree about who should lead in each area of your relationship, it's easy to get along. But deciding who will lead is sometimes tough, especially during a conversation when you both want to lead the discussion and neither is willing to back down and follow. That's often the case when your woman is upset with you and begins an angry discussion by demanding that you apologize for something, whereas you may feel inclined to take control, state your views, and end the discussion.

When she's upset with you and demands an apology, the leadership question is: should you let her lead the conversation or should you take charge?

In an interdependent relationship, it would be odd for one person to *always* lead such discussions, especially since upsetting situations can vary widely. But in practical terms, whoever has more expertise in leading such a discussion will probably end up taking control. That's why it will benefit you to gain expertise in the techniques of strong positive leadership, including conversational leadership.

Chapter by chapter, this book provides strategies and specific techniques to show you how to lead and control the apology-related conversation while avoiding a backlash. Using the techniques presented in this book, you'll learn how to retain your dignity while achieving mutual satisfaction and closure at times when you decide it's best to apologize. You'll also learn about strong positive leadership tactics for handling your woman's emotions and your own during such a conversation. Acquiring these skills will help you become increasingly powerful in your relationship in a way that she will appreciate and admire, and in a way that will make you look and feel more competent, confident, and attractive.

TWO KINDS OF LEADERS

Observing leadership in government, there are at least two kinds of leaders. At one extreme is the all-powerful, authoritarian dictator who rules single-handedly; at the other is the democratically elected president, prime minister, or other head of state who collaborates, compromises, and shares power with other branches of government.

A dictator is typically a strong *negative* leader, exercising leadership by force. His leadership is negative because he frequently enforces decrees that negate the needs and concerns of his people, or of large groups of his people, almost invariably serving primarily his own self-interests – such as staying in power for life. A dictatorial leader may tell himself that his decisions ultimately serve the best interests of his people. Such thoughts reflect the old romanticized concept of philosopher-king. However, as absolute power corrupts absolutely, rarely is there a dictator who is as good and fair as he imagines himself to be. The primary goal of a dictator is to be in complete control and make people do what he tells them to do. He doesn't have to care how the people feel about it as long as they do as they're told. The absolute dictator represents the ultimate "strong man," one who believes that making decisions based on the needs and concerns of others that don't immediately serve his own self-interest is a sign of weakness.

Take North Korean dictator Kim Jong-il as an example. Kim Jong-il makes sure that everybody around him basically remains silent unless they agree with him. As seen on news clips of North Korea, the people there appear to be happy around their "dear leader." But the people don't have personal freedom and are never allowed to openly express their dissenting thoughts and feelings. As long as Kim Jong-il has power, why would he want to hear their complaints? He may believe that he is beloved by his people, but because he silences them, it's doubtful whether they really love him all that much. And it appears that *he* doesn't love *them* very much. If he loved his people, wouldn't he spend more time working to foster economic development so that his people could prosper, and less time garnering public adulation for his own presumed greatness? He appears to love mostly himself.

Think about that for a moment. Some men admire the absolute power of a dictator, but rarely does a man enjoy being bossed around by one, since that involves a loss of personal freedom. Likewise, women who respect themselves don't appreciate losing their freedom of speech and other personal freedoms, either. So in your relationship, if you demand to get your way all the time and silence your woman instead of encouraging her to voice her thoughts and opinions, sooner or later she may love being with you every bit as much as *you* would love being controlled and silenced by a dictator like Kim Jong-il.

An elected leader chosen by the people, on the other hand, generally provides strong *positive* leadership, or leadership by the consent of the governed. It's positive because this kind of leader tries to promote the general welfare of the people and allows them the liberty to live as they choose and pursue happiness on their own terms, generally speaking. If the leader hopes to get reelected and later go down in history as a good leader, he listens to what the people have to say, even when they're upset with him. These heads of state try to promote the growth of individuals, groups, and businesses in their countries so that their economies and cultures will flourish and more citizens will be happy and prosper more of the time. Like any leader, a democratically elected strong positive leader's goal is to maintain control and enjoy great power and influence for the duration of his term. Yet an elected leader can't be too controlling, since that would block individual freedom and the people would turn against him. Such a leader strives for the balance or golden mean between asserting control and encouraging freedom.

Take United States presidents as an example. Unlike a dictator, every U.S. president has tried, to one extent or another, to listen and respond to the people's needs and wishes. These leaders make a lot of strong decisions, but because they're not dictators and must work with co-equal branches of government, they have to be collaborative to some extent, not completely authoritarian. The Founding Fathers designed the U.S. government that way because they firmly believed that power limited by checks and balances is wiser than absolute power. So U.S. presidents must listen to and work with members of Congress, even the ones who disagree with their policies, and they must also abide by the decisions of the Supreme Court. Instead of trying to get the citizens to be quiet and do as they're told, U.S. presidents listen to many different groups and constituencies, government and private sector, as they make decisions in an effort to lead a government of, by, and for the people. Of course, no president is popular with all of the people all of the time since every president has competitors. But it's equally obvious that democratically elected rulers who encourage freedom of speech and action are beloved by more of the people they rule than are absolute dictators who rely on silencing tactics to force their will on their citizens and force a smile on their faces.

Think about what this kind of leadership might mean for you in terms of your relationship. What happens when you use some of the tactics with your woman that strong positive leaders of democracies have used with their people, such as listening, trying to provide solutions and compromises that reasonably satisfy everyone's concerns, and working to ensure freedom and opportunities for others? When you apply these principles to your relationship, you're likely to gain greater appreciation in return. The trade-off is that, unlike a dictator, you can't get your way all the time, and you'll sometimes meet with open complaints and disagreements. But also unlike a dictator, you're less likely to be secretly resented or hated and obeyed out of fear. A strong positive leader is more likely to be followed willingly when followed and praised sincerely when praised.

So within your relationship, a major question for you to consider is this: which kind of leader would you rather emulate? An authoritarian dictator? Or a democratically elected leader?

THE LEADERSHIP POWER PARADOX

This brings us to the paradox of leadership power. We can assume that a strong negative leader like Kim Jong-il wants to believe that he's perceived around the world as among the most powerful leaders alive today. Yet his country is seen as poor, and he's perceived by many as less powerful because of it. By contrast, elected leaders of democratic nations gain influence within their countries by leaving their citizens relatively free to pursue happiness within the framework of the law. Freedom allows a nation to do business and build an economically prosperous country, which, in turn, makes the leader of that nation more powerful and influential, both at home and abroad.

The paradox of leadership power is that, by placing the good of the people above your selfish interests – providing them with rights such as free speech and freedom of assembly as well as the basic resources and reasonable controls they need to achieve their goals and pursue happiness – over time you actually become a more powerful leader on the world stage, not less so. And without being selfish, you get plenty of perks in return. It's a different kind of power than the power of getting your way all the time, as a dictator would. Strong positive leadership brings you a kind of power that resides in the big picture, not in every single detail.

This principle is familiar in the business world, too. As emphasized by experts at the Gallup Organization, corporations and small businesses that focus on keeping their employees engaged by utilizing their talents and strengths create more successful organizations, producing more and better products and services.[3] Those employees are willing to work harder for the company because the company considers their strengths and weaknesses, thoughts and feelings, needs and wants in relation to their work. Ultimately, business leaders benefit when the company turns a greater profit as a result of employee engagement and empowerment.

To lead effectively, leaders on every level need to do a lot of listening. And managerial leaders in particular need to provide constant maintenance – ongoing attention, support, and encouragement – to ensure that their employees remain engaged, growing, and flourishing. Those who don't provide such maintenance tend to lose good people. In fact, it's common knowledge that managers with an especially dictatorial style incur tremendous resentment; self-respecting employees frequently quit or transfer from their jobs to escape them.

The same principle applies to your relationship with a woman. When you promote the interests of your woman from a positive leadership standpoint, she will function at a higher level and give back more in the long run in terms of her excitement, gratitude, and admiration.

Your leadership style can even affect your woman's appearance. For example, if you use a "my way or the highway" approach with your woman, she either struggles with you or just goes along. If she struggles and resists your leadership but usually loses the struggle, she'll look frustrated and angry – not a good look. On the other hand, if she consistently goes along with you, behaving like the proverbial "doormat," some of her potential vivaciousness will remain locked away.

To help your woman look her best, work to listen to her, understand her concerns, and meet her needs and wants in balance with your needs and wants. Offer her as much high quality, appropriate attention as you reasonably can. This will make her more excited to be with you, and her excitement will show in her face and body language. By encouraging her to speak freely and helping her get more of what she wants out of life, you'll actually help her look more attractive.

In fact, if you take a struggling woman and provide her with strong positive leadership, she could end up looking much more attractive over time. That's because receiving strong positive leadership makes people feel more valued than does receiving overly controlling leadership – or no leadership at all. Once she feels more valued, she'll brighten up, and it will be easier to encourage her to cultivate her appearance.

Conversely, if you take a vibrant, attractive woman and treat her as your subject, controlling her and silencing her in a dictatorial way, over the years you would see her beauty transform into anger, bitterness, and cynicism, or perhaps resignation and numbness. A man's leadership style makes a huge difference to his woman's happiness, and sooner or later her appearance reflects it.

So as you begin to master techniques of strong positive leadership, the paradox is that even though you won't get your way in every single situation, overall you'll gain power and influence in your relationship, not lose it – and you'll end up with a relationship that's more exciting.

What does this have to do with apologies? The skill of offering effective apologies when appropriate is a core skill of strong positive leadership. Without an ability to apologize effectively to your woman when truly called for, you'll end up devaluing her – whether you mean to or not – and she will very likely use that against you in the future. Like men, women invariably find ways to strike back when they feel devalued, and if they don't do it consciously they'll do it unconsciously. However, learn the skills surrounding effective apologies and you'll not only avoid blowback but be well on your way to becoming the strong positive leader she'll be increasingly eager to follow.

MORE THAN A LEADER

Apologizing in the right way, at the right time, for the right reason isn't just a key skill for becoming a strong positive leader. At times it can also cast you into the role of hero and healer.

When a woman accuses you of hurting her in some way, she is both asking you to take responsibility for your actions and appealing to you for help. She wants to be rescued from her feeling of being devalued. It's as though she feels you've wounded her, and now she wants you to clean and dress the wound so she can heal. If you inflicted a psychological wound, you are the only person capable of healing that wound in a way that will fully satisfy her. Left unattended, the wound might inspire her to go out on a shopping spree or a drinking binge in an effort to make herself feel better, but at best this can provide only temporary relief. No matter how many nice things she buys for herself or how blasted she gets, in the future she'll still feel totally justified in using your hurtful behavior against you. Or, maybe she could dump you and find somebody else to lick her wounds, in which case she would forever hold your actions against you. That other guy can try all he wants, but he won't be able to heal her in the way that you could.

Not only will the wound you inflicted leave her with an ugly emotional scar, but it will also leave *you* with an *F* on your "relationship report card" in your mind, unless you do something about it. For her, that scar will never fully fade away unless and until you rise to the occasion and provide her with the healing she needs. And for you, being able to bring your failing relationship grade up to an *A* or a *B* will give you new confidence and put you ahead of most other men where relationship skills are concerned.

Before you learn about the skills of apologizing presented in the coming chapters, take a few moments now to complete the self-assessment quiz on the following page. This will give you a baseline profile of the strategies and techniques you currently use to deal with apology-related situations.

Whenever you do or say something that upsets your woman, how do you usually handle it? Do you more or less try to shut her up? Cheer her up? Or do you mix the two strategies?

Self-Assessment Quiz
CHECK ALL THAT APPLY

STRATEGY 1: SHUT-UP TACTICS	STRATEGY 2: CHEER-UP TACTICS
❑ Laugh at her for feeling bad and tell her that she takes things too seriously.	❑ Admit your mistake, express regret, and try to lighten the mood with a smile or a joke.
❑ Let her know she has no right to feel that way and try to prove to her that her feelings are unreasonable.	❑ Listen to her talk about her thoughts/feelings and show understanding and sympathy as you try to make sense of it.
❑ Tell her that if she wants to be with you, she needs to accept you as you are and deal with her feelings on her own.	❑ Reassure her that you care about her feelings and will continue to work hard to understand her perspective.
❑ Stop talking to her, avoid her, or find another way to punish her until she drops the issue.	❑ Take time out to think things over, letting her know you will discuss it again later when you feel calmer.
❑ Point out what she's done in the past to offend you, implying that it's only fair that she should suffer too.	❑ Accept responsibility for your immediate behavior and apologize for the hurt you caused; then acknowledge your lingering resentments and discuss them separately.
❑ Offer to take her out somewhere you want to go, implying that she can take it or leave it and that's as much as you're going to give.	❑ Offer to take her out somewhere she wants to go, giving her the choice as a way of honoring her feelings.
❑ When you think it's not your fault, just say you're sorry so she'll drop it and you won't have to discuss it further; privately chalk up the issue to her stupidity.	❑ When you think it's not your fault, discuss your views honestly, listen to hers with respect, and tell her that even though you don't agree, you still care about her.

Although there are no right or wrong answers, reading this book will give you a clearer idea of how a strong positive leader would ideally handle such situations.

Why apologize? When an apology is called for, look at it as an opportunity to elevate your leadership stature in her eyes. Effective apologies are healing mechanisms that heal her bad feelings and make you look good as well as powerful. Mastering the techniques involved in apologizing effectively is one of the most powerful ways you can boost your score on your internal "relationship report card." More than a leader, you'll go from being a heel to a healer.

How You'll Get There

This book introduces a systematic process for apologizing to your woman when appropriate in a way that will leave her feeling better and leave you looking good. In Chapter 2, you'll learn how to work with two basic dynamics of conversation, especially as they apply to situations that call for an apology. Understanding how to use these conversational dynamics will put you a step ahead, not only in your love relationship but in any relationship. Chapter 3 presents specific steps surrounding an effective apology and explains the importance of the broader process in which an effective apology fits. In Chapter 4, the elements of an apology are shown and demonstrated. Chapters 5 & 6 provide strategies and techniques for handling feelings during an emotional conversation – whether or not an apology is part of the solution. These chapters teach specific techniques that will enable you to turn a conversation around and position yourself as the leader and potential healer, instead of feeling like the victim or the enemy. Chapters 7 & 8 contain examples of typical apologies, both effective and ineffective. You'll learn how some work, some flop, some backfire, and some can be salvaged and brushed up to work better in the future. And you'll see how a woman might hear a particular apology differently than a man does. Finally, Chapter 9 offers tips on what to do after your apology is accepted or rejected, so that you can continue on the path toward greater relationship and leadership success.

THIS BOOK WILL ENABLE YOU TO . . .	SO THAT YOU WILL . . .
Take full responsibility for your actions	➢ Regain her trust ➢ Earn back your right to take charge and lead
Restore her sense of her own value	➢ Regain her approval and appreciation ➢ Be with a more exciting woman
Do the right thing	➢ Like yourself ➢ Help her feel safer and more secure around you
Repair your relationship	➢ Be able to count on her loyalty and cooperation when needed ➢ Be with a happier woman
Increase your relationship competence	➢ Enhance your self-confidence ➢ Win her admiration on a grander scale
Describe the differences between apologies that work and apologies that don't work	➢ Be better equipped to negotiate your relationship with her, and with others as well ➢ Sound smart whenever you give out advice about how to handle a woman's feelings
Turn a difficult situation into a growth opportunity for yourself and for her	➢ Increase your attractiveness ➢ Become a greater force to be reckoned with ➢ Become an impressive role model and leader ➢ Become her hero – and healer

2

HIDDEN DYNAMICS
OF CONVERSATION

All conversations have hidden dynamics. No matter who you're talking to, knowing how to use these dynamics gives you an edge.

In this chapter you'll learn about two hidden dynamics of conversation: *perspective* and *attention*. Using techniques of *perspective* will help you clear up misunderstandings and gain insight into other people, making you a smarter communicator. Using techniques of *attention* will give you more options for getting the results you want from your conversations, including those involving apologies.

The added value of understanding these dynamics is that you'll start to notice how both perspective and attention play out in all sorts of situations. Eventually, you'll discover new ways of using them to benefit yourself in many conversations, both personally and professionally.

Here you'll see how the dynamics of perspective and attention operate from a practical standpoint, specifically when apologizing to your woman. On completing the chapter, you'll understand two of the most basic reasons many apologies fall short of bringing about their desired results.

HIDDEN DYNAMIC #1: OUTER VS. INNER PERSPECTIVE

It's often been said that we rarely see ourselves as others see us. The reason for this comes down to perspectives. From the inside, you "see" yourself based on how it feels to be you and what you think about yourself, as shaped by your personal history and your view of the world. Others see you from outside yourself, based on your appearance, words, and observable behavior within the context of their understandings and worldviews, which could be different from yours.

Have you ever been called a bad name, like *jerk* or *abuser*, and felt that the description was not fair? You might have thought that in spite of how it looked from the outside, there was something right in what you did or said, even if you couldn't explain it.

Or, have you ever called your woman a bad name, like *bitch* or *dope*, and then noticed that she didn't agree with your assessment of her character?

Maybe we're all just a bunch of repressed liars, denying the dirty truths about the lowly depths of our badness and hypocrisy. Or, maybe there's a bigger disconnect than many of us realize between the way we appear to others from the outside and the way we perceive ourselves through our private thoughts and feelings on the inside.

Beneath a person's inner perspective lies a set of motivations for behavior. In any love relationship, motivations are also important to understand. Oddly, some people imagine that they can tell just by looking at someone what motivates him. Occasionally they might be right, but many times people form incorrect conclusions about others because they assume their own life experience, perceptions, and worldview are universally applicable.

By failing to recognize the differences in individual perspectives and the deeper motivations for behavior, people can easily jump to false conclusions about others. For instance, at some point you may think it's not so hard to see what your woman is feeling or thinking right then. She might not be aware of what you see so clearly in her. But even if you're right about her thoughts and feelings, you could still be wrong or confused about what she's aware of and what motivates her. Identifying a person's self-awareness and deeper motivations, which are linked to her thoughts and feelings, isn't always easy, even if you're a perceptive observer.

That's why Sigmund Freud, the father of psychoanalysis and a keenly perceptive man, spent a lot of professional treatment time *listening* to his patients talk. Instead of acting as if he could instantly "psych them out" and then just tell them off to straighten them out, Freud worked hard to understand their inner perspectives as he considered their possible motivations and pieced together a tentative explanation for their behavior.

The truth is that any person's inner perspective is developed through a long personal history, which is more or less hidden from the outer world. A person's motivations for behaving a certain way might be something the person can consciously identify, but isn't always. Sometimes people have no idea why they do certain things. To figure out a person's motivations, you not only need to listen to her but also ask questions, ponder everything you know about her, and plug in your intuition.

Consider for example the large number of possible motivations for telling a lie shown on following chart. A person's motivation for lying may be sinister, but on the other hand it may be as simple as wanting to imitate a childhood role model who happened to behave that way.

Lying

OUTER PERSPECTIVE	POSSIBLE MOTIVATION/INNER PERSPECTIVE
You lie about height or weight or income or IQ	▪ Desire for acceptance/fear of rejection or scorn ▪ Desire to be perceived as socially superior ▪ Fear that your flaws mean something bad about you ▪ Desire to be like your role model, who fibs a lot
You lie about your contact information, such as your address	▪ Desire to be a "private person" ▪ Fear of identity theft ▪ Desire to get away with something ▪ Desire to keep the person out of your life ▪ Desire to avoid the humiliation of admitting you can't remember the information
You lie about something you did, such as spending money, meeting an old friend, or having an affair	▪ Fear of facing your own lack of self-control ▪ Fear of facing the consequences of your actions and the humiliation it would bring ▪ Fear of dealing with bigger problems related to it ▪ Fear of hurting others unnecessarily ▪ Desire to remain childlike and get something for nothing, along with the thrill of the risk ▪ Desire to break a rule for the sake of rebellion and self-assertiveness ▪ Desire to get even with someone
You lie by giving false compliments/flattery	▪ Desire to disguise your disdain or pity for the person you're complimenting ▪ Desire to be generous ▪ Desire to get others' money or sexual favors ▪ Desire to be accepted and appear charming ▪ Desire to be just like someone else who acts that way
You lie outrageously, hoping or expecting to be caught	▪ Desire to take the spotlight off someone else to protect that person from being caught in a misdeed ▪ Desire to send up a red flag signaling a deeper problem that you don't know how to verbalize ▪ Desire to attract attention and get appropriate discipline from a parent/authority figure who is neglecting his disciplinary role ▪ Desire to grab headlines in society at any cost
You lie to outwit	▪ Desire to be cute, clever, and amusing ▪ Desire to get even for a previous wrong ▪ Desire to make a fool out of others as a subtle way of expressing your contempt for them ▪ Desire to see yourself as superior to others ▪ Desire to be just like a parent or other role model ▪ Desire to cheat others for material gain ▪ Desire to compete with others who also outwit ▪ Desire to escape from being trapped or enslaved

The point here is that it's often a mistake to jump to conclusions about people's inner perspectives (what they think is true) and their motivations (why they do what they do). Lying is a behavior that might be perceived by others – an outer perception, and might also be perceived by the speaker – an inner perception. However, people's *motivations* to lie grow out of their fears and desires, bound up with perceptions, thoughts, feelings, and attitudes shaped through a unique personal history, as well as their assessments and expectations of the world. The motivations for any person's behavior may be straightforward, or they may be complicated by convoluted thinking and misperceptions based on a history of being abused.

Sharing Perspectives

In a close personal relationship with a woman, her thoughts, feelings, and motivations are important for you to try to understand, just as it's important for her to understand your inner world to some extent. That's part of how people bond with each other. The bond you create is the glue that holds together your relationship. Your shared insights into one another's perspectives – thoughts and feelings based on each of your unique histories and worldviews – amplify your understanding of yourselves and each other. This process is crucial to building and maintaining trust and to reducing feelings of loneliness.

For many couples at the beginning of a relationship, that kind of understanding seems to come naturally. Your intuition or keen insight or gut feeling may lead you to believe you know what's motivating your partner or what's bothering her. But as time goes by, you may occasionally feel confused by the way she acts or by a look on her face that doesn't seem to fit your image of her. She may feel the same kind of confusion about you, too. Even when you try your best, you probably don't always know what's going on in her mind.

Of course, you shouldn't be *expected* to read her mind because *you're not her*. And furthermore, how much do you really *need* to know or share? When she corners you and starts to give you a complete accounting of all the scattered things she's been thinking, or when she unloads a bundle of bad feelings on you, you might wish you didn't have to hear about her inner perspective, especially before she has it sorted out. You probably try to control *your* feelings in a self-sufficient way, sorting them out before verbalizing them, and you may wonder why she doesn't do the same. Furthermore, when she urges you to disclose your private thoughts and feelings on *her* timetable, you might feel that your privacy is being invaded.

What she understands is that sharing inner perspectives is critical for keeping your love alive and ensuring that you don't drift apart. What she doesn't necessarily understand is how to lead the conversation so that the timing and flow of conversation are right for both of you. She's an eager relationship participant in need of a conversational leader, and that leader ought to be you – once you learn how.

Anger: Perspectives and Interventions

An important step in becoming a conversational leader in your relationship is learning to identify and handle women's feelings. Let's take some time now to consider a common feeling where apologies are concerned: anger. When you see or suspect that your woman is mad at you, the first thing you have to figure out is why: what's causing her anger? If you jump to conclusions and guess that she's just putting on an act, whereas she's really not, you might hurt her feelings and add another level of anger to have to handle with an apology. Then again, if you were to automatically take her anger seriously in a situation where she was just manipulating you by throwing a tantrum to get her way, then you could be played for a fool.

The following chart describes expressions of anger and interventions for handling them. In the left-hand column you'll see a few diverse experiences that your woman could be expressing when she gets angry, along with the behavior you'll observe that helps you determine what she's experiencing. In the right-hand column, you'll see intervention strategies. These concepts will be revisited in greater detail in Chapter 6.

Anger

INNER EXPERIENCE/ OUTER BEHAVIOR	INTERVENTION
A momentary feeling that she expresses immediately of being slighted; she tells you that she's hurt or angry about something specific.	Listen to her complaint and figure out (or ask) what you said or did that made her feel devalued, and in what way she feels devalued. Then give her appropriate attention and address the issue(s) concerned to help her feel valued again.
A cascade of over-whelming, painful emotions stemming from something specific that happened to her that she feels has seriously devalued her; she is extremely upset and can't calm down, as feelings continue to surface.	Help her uncover, layer by layer, the painful emotions and related thoughts buried under the anger until you bring her focus of attention down to whatever positive desire, longing, or dream is hidden beneath the pain. Then coach her to build a more realistic new strategy for achieving in the present or future that positive thing she desires, longs for, or dreams of. She needs new hope that her dream can still come true.
An intellectual expectation and firm belief that some event in the recent or distant past or over the course of a lifetime should have been different than it was; she keeps asking *why?*	Help her identify her past expectations. Then help her rethink and retroactively change her expectations in light of the reality of the situation as it now appears. Next, help her generate new hope around developing a more realistic strategy for getting the love, attention, or whatever she expected and thought she should have gotten in the past.
A calculated strategy of throwing a self-righteous tantrum so that others would rush around and try to please her – an act she uses to get whatever she wants, which she learned as a child when her personality was being formed; she manipulates you, trying every trick imaginable to get her way.	Call her on her act by being firm and confident, like a bemused adult catching a two-year-old in the act of trying to fool the grownups. If what she wants is reasonable, explain that pouts and tantrums won't work, but that she can get what she wants if she is willing to act more grown up. Teach her the steps she needs to take to do so, and give her a chance to succeed by being more mature. Do this with patience and insistence but without harsh blame, since she may view blame as a game and try to use it against you, or disregard everything you say because of your tone. If what she wants is unreasonable, help her learn what is reasonable for her to get and what steps she needs to take to get it.
A sense that one of her boundaries has been crossed or that she has been seriously insulted; she goes silent to command your attention and obtain whatever she demands.	Ask questions, listen to her demands, and take action. If her demands are reasonable, you should honor them and apologize for your mistake. If not, ask questions and learn about her perspectives until you identify the underlying issue(s). Then apply the appropriate intervention (above right) for her anger experience (above left).

Why All the Fuss?

You might wonder why relationships have to be so complicated. Maybe you think that if you know what you did wrong in a particular situation and if you say you're sorry, then you shouldn't have to talk about motivations, thoughts, feelings, and all that junk. Of course, that's true in many cases, when the thing you're apologizing for isn't a big deal to your woman or when she's able to get over it.

But as you probably know from experience, there are times when this straightforward approach falls short. She may demand to know *why* you did what you did and then reject the answer you give her. Or, it may turn out that she's actually upset about something else related to what you did or said. Maybe it's not *what* you said but *the way* you said it. Or maybe something you said or did reminds her of something completely random.

Talking at length about their thoughts and feelings often enables women to process their experiences. By listening and responding in certain ways, you can help your woman. If you learn how to grasp her emotionally charged, imaginative inner perspective and lead her toward a positive conclusion to the conversation, you can save yourself a lot of grief – and help her appreciate you more. Also, whenever she talks about her thoughts and feelings in a situation where you don't owe an apology, just being aware of her inner perspective will help you ask the right questions, know what to listen for, and efficiently steer the conversation to a peaceful conclusion.

For now, remember this: in a situation where your woman is seriously upset and you're not completely clear on why, it's usually a mistake to try to use a quick apology to end the conversation without first understanding her inner perspective as much as possible. That's because, if you don't take the time to understand her fully, you may later lose control of the conversation when she springs more of her thoughts and feelings on you after you thought you were done.

The best way to maintain conversational control when you feel you owe an apology is to gather enough information from your woman *before* apologizing so that you know just what to apologize *for*. Depending on the situation, you may also need to keep gathering information from her during your apology-based conversation so that you can remain in control. Later on, you'll see how this works.

HIDDEN DYNAMIC #2: ATTENTION

Women and men both crave attention but tend to pursue it in different ways. Many men care about their appearance and personality, and yet with women they often seek attention mainly for their career, their accomplishments, their wealth, their possessions, their social influence, and their favorite activities. Too much personal attention may feel uncomfortable to them, even in their love relationships. Although many women also seek and appreciate attention for their careers, activities, possessions, and accomplishments, the kinds of attention women tend to appreciate most in love relationships include attention to their personality, their appearance, their taste and style, their home, and their relationship savvy. However, these are just general tendencies. Furthermore, individual men and women sometimes have very particular ideas about types of attention they want most and have their own unique ways of seeking them.

Wherever attention is craved, there is great power for those who would satisfy that craving.

Attention takes many forms. The skill of giving appropriate attention strategically, whether you need to apologize or at any other time, is probably the single most powerful tool at your disposal for being successful in personal relationships. Especially in a situation where you choose to offer an apology, it's important to know techniques for directing appropriate attention so that your apology works to your advantage.

When people receive attention, it often feels like love. From the time when, as a child, you first rode your bike and shouted, "Hey Mom, look at me!" to the time when, as an adult, you hoped a particular woman was looking at you as you subtly shifted your eyes in response to her, getting the attention you want and feel you deserve has been central to your happiness.

Likewise, the more attention you give your woman in ways she finds desirable, and the more different forms of desirable attention you provide, the more she'll feel that you love her. Having the power of attention means having many little ways of expressing love to your woman that she will appreciate, thereby earning credit toward more of the forms of attention you want from her in return. All you need to do is learn to harness the power of attention-giving that already lies within you.

Some of the ways a man traditionally pays attention to a woman are:

- Saying: "You're beautiful" and similar compliments
- Bringing her flowers, candy, jewelry, or other gifts
- Inviting her out to dinner, a show, a party, or other social event
- Listening to her talk about her opinions and interests

More ways of paying attention to your woman that are fairly simple and low cost include the following:

- Give her eye contact when you talk.
- Gaze into her eyes when you're alone together.
- Watch her from a distance to appreciate her appearance or her spirit, and wait until she notices you're looking.
- When you're together, let her know nonverbally what you like about her.
- Touch her in a nice way.
- Carefully watch her moment-by-moment experience of an event.
- Share out loud your positive interests and desires related to her.
- Ask her to share her thoughts, opinions, feelings, concerns, worries, hopes, and dreams.
- Notice the way she looks and dresses and wears her hair and encourage what you like about it.
- Look for one nice thing about her that you didn't notice before and make a casual remark about it.
- Joke with her gently to lighten her mood, when needed.
- Learn which activities are fun for her and do them with her more often, or encourage her to do them with friends.
- Encourage her to develop herself in the ways she wants to grow.

Tips from Relationship Experts

In his landmark book, *How to Win Friends and Influence People*, Dale Carnegie described many ways of giving positive attention to others. Paraphrasing his advice in terms of your relationship with your woman, here are a few of Carnegie's suggestions:

- Smile at her.
- Say her name frequently.
- Show interest in her when you talk.
- Ask her about her interests.
- Let her do a great deal of talking.
- Listen well as you encourage her to talk about herself.
- Try to see things from her viewpoint.
- Be sympathetic to her thoughts and desires.
- If you criticize her, preface it with praise and appreciation.
- Rather than finding fault, ask her to do what you want her to do and provide encouragement as she changes.
- Let her know she's important to you.
- Show respect for her opinions, whether or not you agree with them.
- When you're wrong, admit it.[4]

These simple recommendations will go a long way toward making your woman feel loved.

Another source of ideas for giving your woman a wider range of appropriate attention to help her feel loved is Stephen Covey's *The 7 Habits of Highly Effective People*. In his "Paradigms of Interdependence" chapter, Covey talks about building up an "Emotional Bank Account" by making six major types of "deposits." These "deposits," paraphrased in terms of giving attention to your woman, are as follows:

- Work hard to understand her; spend time listening carefully to get to know what's important to her; honor whatever she considers important as a way of showing that you value her.
- Be kind and courteous, knowing that in a relationship with your woman, small courtesies – as well as discourtesies – may be big things to her.

- Keep your word with her.
- Clarify your respective roles and goals.
- Apply the same principles to her that you apply to yourself, and don't say things about her behind her back that you wouldn't say to her face.
- Apologize sincerely to regain her trust whenever you make a "bank account withdrawal" by being rude, breaking a promise, etc.[5]

Appropriate vs. Inappropriate

Men sometimes think that paying a compliment is the best way to give a woman attention. However, to a woman, compliments only feel loving when they seem appropriate. Sometimes positive attention feels wrong, or downright weird. Think of how you feel when someone watches you at length for no apparent reason. Or constantly flatters you. Not good, right? So what exactly makes attention *appropriate* – or *not*?

You might think the answer is obvious: you can just tell. When she gives you attention, it's easy to tell whether it's appropriate by how it feels to receive it.

True enough. Unfortunately, though, when you give what *you* feel is appropriate attention to her, she might not agree that your actions or words feel appropriate. The Golden Rule doesn't always apply in determining what kinds of attention are appropriate to give to others. That's because of the differences in individual perspectives.

When it comes to giving your woman attention, her inner perspective – thoughts and feelings based on her unique history and worldview – is probably not the same as yours. In fact, her inner experience of a certain type of attention could be quite different than your inner experience would be if she paid that kind of attention to you. Therefore, the kinds of attention *you* like to get might not be the kinds of attention *she* wants to get. In addition, every individual is a little bit different, which means not all women are alike; the kinds of attention other women in your past seemed to appreciate may not be exactly the same as the kinds of attention the woman in your life today prefers.

Ultimately, to have the effect of giving love, the attention you give your woman has to feel appropriate *to her*.

When Positive Attention Feels Wrong

Here's an example of how bad it can feel to get positive attention that's inappropriate. Imagine that you were a normal kid growing up in a normal neighborhood. The other kids treated you as an equal, more or less. But as you got older, your family became far wealthier than everyone else in your area, and all of a sudden the kids started treating you very, very well. You knew you were still the same regular guy, but when your family got more money, people seemed overly complimentary. In this scenario, wouldn't you get a funny feeling that they were being nice to you because maybe they wanted your money? You might feel a little weird and wish that nobody knew your family had money so that you could go back to being just one of the guys. Essentially, people would be giving you attention that is too positive. It would make you uncomfortable and lonely to think that nobody was being real with you. You could even become cynical about humanity, as some people do when they win the lottery and their friends and relatives suddenly start buttering them up, or old acquaintances pop out of the woodwork acting like long-lost best friends.

That's similar to how a woman feels when she's just being a regular nice person and, maybe because of her pretty face or figure, a man showers her with too much positive attention. Compliments feel fabulous to her when she believes they're deserved, but too many compliments seem weird. She might get a funny feeling that the man just wanted to use her for the "riches" he could get from her. This would be especially true if he doesn't want to hear about her inner perspective or share his honest inner perspective with her, as those who really love each other do. His excessive positive attention would eventually make her feel uncomfortable and lonely, and could also make her feel cynical about men.

Here's another example: imagine that as a kid, you were a favored child, allowed to break a lot of rules and always get away with it, both at home and at school. In fact, you were treated as if you could do no wrong: your every mistake or bad behavior was overlooked, explained away, or readily forgiven. Imagine that your parents were needy people who idealized you, constantly trying to please you in the hopes that you would fill their overwhelming need for love. If that were true, you'd grow up continuing to break rules, thinking it was fun and funny and suspecting that adults were pretty stupid. You'd develop contempt for the foolishness of others but unconsciously hope that your parents (or the adult world) would wise up and discipline you. You might develop a sense of over-confidence and privileged entitlement, think you're smarter than everyone else, and feel contemptuous of the "dorky," rule-abiding "losers" and "chumps" all around you. Not only would you think you were better than others, but somewhere inside you'd also feel angry and cynical toward the world for not seeing you as the person you really were.

That's similar to what a woman feels when a man is overly accepting and fails to provide negative attention when it's appropriate, whether it's because he's needy and afraid of not pleasing her or because his mind is elsewhere most of the time. Given no oversight, she might overspend and overindulge, or get lazy and give less, and seem from the outside to be enjoying these self-indulgences. Deep inside, she would feel lonely and frustrated by his lack of appropriate attention, including appropriate negative, boundary-setting attention. However, in her interactions, she might easily develop cynicism toward him and believe herself to be superior and entitled to whatever she wants.

To find out whether your woman feels that the attention you offer her is appropriate, here are some simple ideas:

- When you give her some form of attention, watch her reaction. If it's not what you expect or if it seems to be more of an act or formality on her part than a genuine response, don't take it personally. Just realize that the attention you gave her may not be a form of attention she values greatly.

- Ask her what kinds of attention she enjoys most, doesn't really want, and dreams of getting. Maybe the attention you've been giving her isn't registering with her the way you thought. You might learn some simple ways to give her more of the kinds of attention she wants.

- Ask her whether she feels she's getting enough attention from you, overall, and if not, ask her to elaborate. Then silently consider how much attention you think you give her vs. how much she seems to feel she receives from you. Finally, imagine different forms of attention that you could try out, possibly including boundary-setting attention, in an effort to help her feel more loved.

By keeping your eyes and ears open and asking her some simple questions, you may learn a lot of handy information that will help you score points with her in the future. The more time and thought you put in to giving her the kinds of attention she appreciates most, the sooner you can develop a strategy for leveraging your attention-giving initiatives to get more of the kinds of attention you want from her in return.

Control and Manipulation

Because giving attention has the power to make people feel liked and loved, it can be used by those who want to control you, whether it's overt control or subtle manipulation. In other words, people often give you attention so that you will do something for them in return, whether their goal is mutual friendship, legitimate control, or self-centered manipulation.

On the legitimate side, friends pay attention to friends expecting an equal exchange of good will. Managers and bosses at work give their workers attention as a way of motivating them and helping them do their jobs more effectively. Workers give their managers and bosses attention to stay employed, learn what to do, and attract promotions and raises. Salespeople give customers and prospective customers attention because they want them to buy their products and services. Customers and prospects give salespeople attention to the extent that they see a benefit in the products and services on offer, or when they enjoy getting attention from that particular salesperson and so want the association to continue. Teachers give their students attention to encourage and instruct them, help them overcome challenges, and control their behavior. Students give teachers attention to stay out of trouble, get good grades, get the teacher's approval, and learn the subject matter.

On the illegitimate side, scam artists give innocent bystanders positive, flattering attention that they try to pass off as appropriate because they're priming them to give up their money. Pedophiles as well as sexual predators in the adult world give extremely intense, positive attention to those they intend to victimize, often staring hypnotically into their eyes in order to create inappropriate bonds and flatter them with extreme attention, thereby gaining control. A woman might give a man attention to fool him into thinking that she really likes or loves him, so that he will do things for her in

29

the hopes of one day being able to score. Men may use the same treatment on women: a man might fool a woman into believing he's fascinated by her so that he can get what he wants from her whenever he wants it. In the workplace, legitimate forms of attention to gain appropriate control and acts of self-centered manipulation are often intermingled and sometimes confused for personal love. In and out of the workplace, men and women flirt to snag each other's admiring attention in the moment, regardless of what they privately think of each other.

The act of giving personal attention is potentially very powerful. When giving your attention to someone, be sure to consider your motivations carefully, because if she decides your motives are not legitimate, she's likely to use your words and actions against you in the future.

Learning to give your woman appropriate attention in a greater variety of forms based on legitimate motivations will help you strengthen your relationship and, in Covey's language, build up your "Emotional Bank Account" with her. Having a healthy "account balance" will give you greater opportunities to get more of what you want from her in return.

To harness the power of attention-giving as it relates to an apology, now it's time to drill down and examine in detail how attention flows in a typical verbal exchange. Specifically, you'll see how to track the flow of attention in a brief conversation and learn a technique for consciously steering your focus of attention during an apology to increase your chances of success.

THE FOCUS TRIANGLE

What is focus? In this book, *focus* refers to *focus of attention*.

In a conversation, *focus* is a concept related to *topic*, but slightly different. The *topic* is whatever you're discussing, whereas the *focus* is the place where your attention goes from moment to moment as you discuss the topic.

Below is a simple diagram called the *Focus Triangle*.[6] The Focus Triangle is a learning model I created and co-developed for describing conversational skills. It tracks the moment-by-moment flow of attention and shows participants' perspectives — thoughts, feelings, and value judgments — during a conversation in progress.

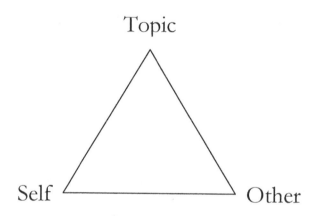

The Focus Triangle shows that any topic can be discussed from three basic directions:

1. Talking about yourself in relation to the topic (*Self* focus)
2. Talking about the other person in relation to the topic (*Other* focus)
3. Talking about the topic as it might be understood from an impersonal, objective, fact-based viewpoint (*Topic* focus)

Choosing the right focus will help you succeed when you need to apologize. Conversely, choosing the wrong focus can block your success. You might be truly sorry for something you did or said, and you might think you're saying all the right words. Yet if your conversational focus during an apology flows in the wrong direction, you won't get the best results.

Tracking the Focus

Imagine that you're talking to your woman about the milk she drinks at breakfast. *Milk* is the topic. If you use a Topic focus, you make an objective statement about milk, such as: "Here's the milk."

On the Focus Triangle, the Topic focus for the statement: "Here's the milk" is tracked by circling the top angle of the triangle.

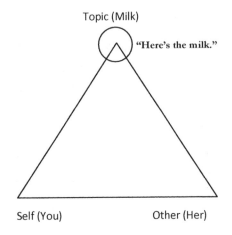

Next, you decide to express your dislike of milk: "Milk is for *babies*. Yuck."

Your topic is still milk. Your statement (A) "Milk is for..." sounds like it's going to be an objective statement. But by using a put-down tone of voice when you say (B) "babies" and by adding "yuck" at the end, you've turned your statement into

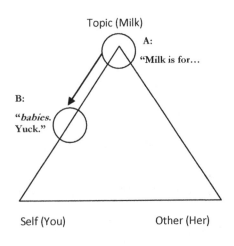

a personal opinion. Your focus of attention falls to somewhere between yourself and the topic. That's because, by giving your personal commentary on the topic, your opinion draws attention toward you.

Now, imagine that the woman you're talking to responds with: "Hey now, that's not right! A lot of people drink milk and really like it – including me!" Below, you can see how your focus of attention based on her comments quickly shifts around on your Focus Triangle.

In her statement, the woman first refers to your opinion by saying: (A) "Hey now! That's not right!" Then she draws your attention to a factual claim by saying: (B) "A lot of people drink milk and really like it." This moves your attention up to a Topic focus. Finally, when she says: (C) "including me!" she suddenly brings the conversational focus to herself. Her comments have changed the focus but not the topic, since she's still basically talking about milk.

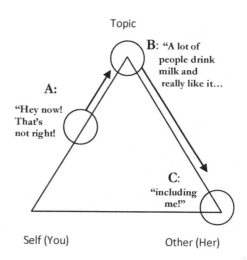

Topic

B: "A lot of people drink milk and really like it…

A: "Hey now! That's not right!

C: "including me!"

Self (You)   Other (Her)

Your Focus Triangle vs. Hers

In an actual conversation between two people, each person identifies with the word *Self* and calls the other person *Other*. So when tracking a conversation, it sometimes helps to draw and label two separate Focus Triangles, one for each person.

As you can see below, if you said, "Milk is for *babies*. Yuck," your comments would show up one way on *your* Focus Triangle (left), and in mirror image on *her* Focus Triangle (right).

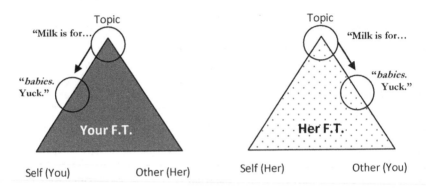

Also, in real-world conversations, people sometimes have different *interpretations* of where the focus lies at any given moment. For instance, when you say, "Milk is for *babies*. Yuck," she might hear you as self-important, and think that your comments draw attention closer to *you* than to the *topic*. Yet you hear yourself as mostly objective. When that happens, your respective Focus Triangles are no longer mirror images.

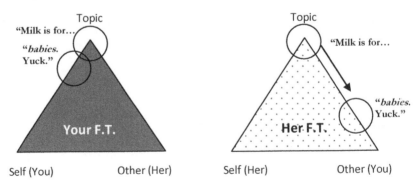

Positive and Negative Values

A major feature of the Focus Triangle is the *value* given to each angle: Topic, Self, and Other. People have good, bad, or neutral feelings about themselves, the people they talk to, and the things they talk about. Emotional sparks are a natural part of many conversations, since it's only human to judge people and things as good, bad, or indifferent and to sometimes express these value judgments.

On a Focus Triangle, positive and negative values are shown by the plus (+) and minus (-) signs. A neutral value is shown by the tilde (~).

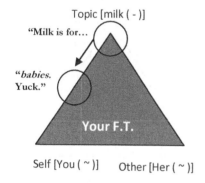

When you said, "Milk is for *babies. Yuck,*" you brought the conversational *focus* from the topic to somewhere between yourself and the topic, but at the same time you gave milk a negative *value*. However, you felt you made an innocent statement. You didn't mean anything negative about *her*.

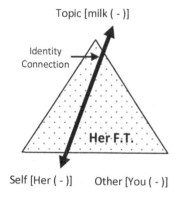

What you didn't realize is that since she loved milk, she identified with it. When you put milk down, she felt put down, too. In her mind, the fact that you made this comment showed that you either didn't remember that she loved milk, which meant you weren't paying enough attention to even *know* her, or else you were just being rude. She immediately judged you negatively.

Since both men and women identify strongly with the things they love, they feel that their value is connected to the value of those things. Whenever someone makes a negative comment about that topic, the listener's Self value goes negative too. For example, if you love baseball and somebody trashes the sport, you'd probably have strong feelings about their comments. In the language of the Focus Triangle, that's called an *Identity Connection*. For the listener, the focus of the conversation isn't just the topic, but both the topic and himself. The listener feels as though he is being talked about quite personally when that topic is discussed.

By saying: "Hey now! That's not right! A lot of people drink milk and really like it – including me!" your woman flipped the value of both the topic and herself back to positive on her Focus Triangle. At the same time, she viewed you as negative for insulting her.

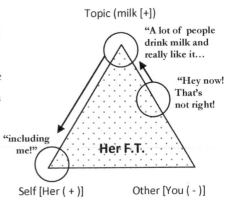

Now, you realize that, for some reason, she's upset with you. Her reaction plus her rejection of your opinion of milk make you feel ticked off. You still think milk is bad, but now you also see her as bad for making you feel that you don't have a right to state your opinion. Your values of milk and of her are now negative, and your Self value has also gone negative because you're mad.

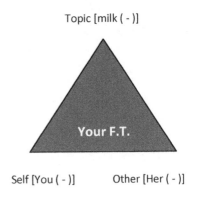

At this point, you're confronted with a challenging situation. First, you disagree about the value of milk. To feel better, either you both need to accept your separate opinions amicably or one of you needs to persuade the other so that you agree. More importantly, you now feel that your own value has been diminished by her, just as she felt a moment earlier that her value was diminished by you. Since all people need to feel good about themselves, you'll have to find a way to make your Self value go back to positive. Finally, you're confused about why she got upset in the first place and you begin to wonder about her value: is she really as good as you thought?

WHAT TO DO?

In an effort to steer the conversation so that you can recapture good feelings, you'll probably try one of three basic approaches:

1. A *self-centered approach*: you say things to make *yourself* feel better (to make your Self on your Focus Triangle flip back from negative to positive).
2. An *other-centered approach*: you say things to try to make *her* feel better (to make her Self on her Focus Triangle go back to positive), which will then help you feel better.
3. A *topic-centered approach*: you ignore all feelings and argue factually about milk's objective merits and demerits to determine the "objective truth" (as if there were one): whether milk is really a good drink or a bad one. (This will make your Self on your Focus Triangle flip back from negative to positive *if and only if* you win the argument.)

A Self-centered Approach

If you zero in on how bad you feel and decide to say things to try to make yourself feel better, you're taking a self-centered approach. Many people instinctively understand that being self-centered is often a good thing. In fact, to meet your own needs, it's essential and healthy to focus on yourself much of the time. But is this the best approach to use when your woman is upset?

In any conversation where someone has made you feel bad for the moment, taking a self-centered approach might lead you to handle the situation using one or more of the following focuses:

♦ A positive Self focus in which you defend your goodness and positive value

♦ A negative Other focus in which you put the other person down to feel better by comparison

♦ An opinion focus in which you argue that your opinion is better or more valuable than the other person's opinion

The self-centered approach is designed to save yourself, not necessarily to hurt anyone else – unless of course you *have* to hurt someone else to save yourself (ha ha) – or unless hurting someone else seems to be the quickest and easiest way to feel better (ha ha).

In our example, imagine that when your woman said, "Hey now, that's not right..." you took her remarks as a personal criticism for speaking out – as if she were saying that you were *wrong* just for expressing a heartfelt opinion about milk that she didn't happen to agree with. Whether or not you noticed that she felt bad too, your main concern from a self-centered standpoint would be making yourself feel better again as soon as possible, since her criticism left you feeling slighted.

♦ You might wonder, "Gee whiz, why can't I just be honest about my opinions?! How come I always have to listen to *her* opinions, but yet when I share *mine* it causes a big problem?" (That's a negative Self focus flipped positive by using a "poor me" tone. By appealing for sympathy, you imply that you're really good. The woman appears to be unfair, which at that moment gives her a negative value on your Focus Triangle, whereas you believe you're good because you feel that you're an innocent victim of conversational gender discrimination.)

♦ You might respond by saying nothing out loud and trying to act tough and cool. (That's a positive Self-focused behavior: you're drawing attention to yourself nonverbally to impress her with how tough and cool you look.)

- You might say nothing but silently think to yourself, "Women! They always have to get their way, even though they're dumb." (That's a negative Other-focused thought. You feel good compared to women, who you think are selfish and dumb.)

- You might say out loud, "Oh, Okay," as you grin and roll your eyes at her and appreciate yourself for being cleverly sarcastic. (The verbal focus is on her opinion but the nonverbal focus is on you. You flip your Self value to positive because you give yourself credit for being clever and avoiding a confrontation. It's also negative Other focused: verbally you approve of her opinion, but rolling your eyes shows that you think her opinion is bad, making your Other value go negative.)

- You might deny her opinion by saying, "No, *you're* wrong! Milk is totally yucky." (That's a negative Other focus followed by an opinion focus, which you use to try to nullifying her criticism of your opinion so that you can feel better. Your assertion flips her value – your Other – negative on your Focus Triangle to the extent that you think her opinion isn't as good as yours, and at the same time it flips your Self value positive because you feel your opinion is better.)

- You might counter her opinion with a positive assertion such as, "I have a right to my opinion, don't I?" (That's a positive Self focus, asserting your right to state your opinion, which implies that you're good, not bad, for doing so.)

No matter which lines you use, employing a self-centered strategy will give you a brief ego boost as you flip your Self value from negative to positive on your own Focus Triangle. It's like the sugar rush you get when you eat a piece of candy: it may do harm in the long run, but at the moment it gives you a blast of good feeling.

Unfortunately, in a relationship conflict – even a very minor one – the problem with taking a self-centered approach is that it sets in motion continued conflict. The question in your mind: "Why can't a man express his honest opinions to a woman, even though she can express hers to him?" creates an inner conflict that will continue to bother you indefinitely, as long as you believe the rules of conversation are slanted in favor of women. Your tough and cool act will leave your woman hanging, so that she'll continue to struggle with you to switch the conversational focus to herself until you help her feel better, or else she'll get mad and start caring a little less what you think. Your private thought that women are unfair and dopey will put you into long-term, low-level inner turmoil as you realize that you need and want the love of someone you believe is unfair and dopey – and it will leave your woman hanging in the conversation. Also, if ever she senses that you harbor these negative judgments about women, tensions between you would likely erupt. Your sarcastic eye rolling is likely to tempt your woman to get even with you at some point, thus continuing the struggle between the two of you. Of course, this can be lighthearted banter, but as the years go by lighthearted banter sometimes turns hurtful. Telling her bluntly that she's wrong or insisting that you have a right to your opinion may either spark a longer argument or shut her down. Shutting her down will fuel her inner resentment, which she will unleash on you sometime in the future.

The point is that using a self-centered response during a relationship conflict, however minor the conflict may be, generally breeds further conflict, either between the two of you or internally within one of you.

An Other-centered Approach

If you focus on how the other person feels and you want to help her feel better, you're taking an other-centered approach. An other-centered approach to conversation is very useful whenever you already feel good and confident about yourself.

To deliver other-centered remarks successfully, it's critical that you feel confident, or at least generally okay about yourself. You have to feel self-accepting before you can have something positive to give. Using an other-centered approach in an apology when you feel bad about yourself tends to fail, even if you manage to come up with all the "right words." That's because your negative feelings about yourself come across nonverbally whether you know it or not, sending a mixed message.

In a conversation with your woman when you notice that her Self value has gone negative, taking an other-centered approach leads you to handle the situation using one or more of the following techniques:

♦ A positive Other focus, in which you say something nice to her about herself

+ A neutral Self focus or a slightly altered opinion focus, in which you explain yourself in a responsible but non–self-blaming way, carefully rephrasing whatever you said that made her feel bad by restating it as you meant to say it, so that it's no longer insulting

+ An opinion focus, in which you discuss an opinion *she* has expressed, asking questions to further explore her views and experiences rather than interjecting your views and opinions, thus giving her positive attention by interviewing her about her inner perspective and showing interest in it

+ A negative Self focus, if done in an engaging and lighthearted tone*

*Note that some men will put themselves down in an effort to negate the hurt they've caused or to make the woman feel better by comparison. This can work well if delivered with a sense of humor, because humor conveys an underlying strength and self-confidence. However, it will backfire if it makes the woman feel that she then has to help the man feel better about himself. The problem with using a negative Self focus is that it assumes the woman will enjoy seeing the man look bad. This puts her in an odd position if, in general, she wants to believe in him and admire him. Unless delivered in a lighthearted tone, a negative Self-focused comment, such as "I am such a clod!" makes a man sound weak.

An other-centered approach is ideal for rescuing your woman from feeling bad because of something you've said or done. Delivered with confidence and sincerity, it helps both of you feel better – she because you've helped her, and you because you've done a good job of helping her.

Scenario 1

When your woman protests, "Hey now, that's not right…" imagine that you immediately realize she feels put down by your opinion of milk, although at first you aren't sure why.

Then, when she says, "…including me!" it dawns on you that she loves milk and that your comment about milk has just insulted her. Instead of feeling bad for saying something wrong or for forgetting that she's a big milk drinker, you decide that your slip-up was a simple mistake, not the end of the world, and you feel confident that all you have to do now is help her feel better and then everything will be all right. You want to make her feel better – not out of a sense of shame or excessive guilt, but because you care about her and you think it's the right thing to do under the circumstances. Therefore, you take responsibility for the slip-up and apologize. Thanks to your keen insight into her inner perspective, here's what you say:

- ◆ "Oh, sorry, I didn't mean to criticize your taste! You're right, you know, a lot of people of all ages love milk, and I guess there's nothing wrong with that. I just can't stand milk myself, that's all – but I definitely like you, even if you are a milk drinker! I should have said: 'Milk is for babies . . . *and* for *babes!*'"

Here, you admit your mistake, express regret, and stick to your honest opinion of milk while modifying the way you say it so as not to be insulting. You also make her feel loved again by helping her see a clear distinction between milk, which you don't like, and her, who you do like. This helps her separate her value as a woman, which you support, from the value of milk, which she values but you don't, although you allow that it's perfectly normal to value it. Finally, you end with a light-hearted compliment.

This approach allows you to fix the problem, maintain your honest negative opinion of milk rather than backing down, help her feel better, and make yourself look good in the process. It's a win-win.

Scenario 2

Now imagine that you don't know for sure whether she feels hurt by your "yuck" comment, but when she comes back with her "Hey now, that's not right..." comment, you can tell she's having some kind of a negative reaction. You feel good about noticing this because you know it means you're paying attention. You decide to just *ask* her what she feels, and she tells you that she feels insulted by your "yuck" comment because she loves milk. From that information, you realize that your negative opinion of milk made her feel insecure. Out of care and concern for her feelings and a willingness to take responsibility for accidentally insulting her, you put together an other-centered apology. Turning the conversational focus to her in a neutral or positive way, your goals are to take away her hurt feelings and win points for being a gentleman. Here's what you say:

♦ "Say there, I just noticed that you seemed to feel uncomfortable when I said that I can't stand milk. How did it make you feel when I said that?" [Insulted, because I love milk!] "Whoa. I didn't mean to do that. Sorry. My mistake. I forgot that milk was so important to you. By the way, how much milk do you drink in a week? [Up to a gallon]. Really? Well, there must be something good about milk then, because it seems to do good things for you."

Instead of dwelling on your negative opinion of milk or backing down from it, you simply move away from focusing on your opinion to focusing on her. You politely admit your mistake and express sincere regret without feeling bad about it (Sorry. My mistake.); disclose your motives (I forgot that milk was so important to you); and shift to asking her more about her milk consumption (By the way...). Your apology ends by focusing positive attention on milk and on her. This makes her feel better, and the negative Self value on her Focus Triangle immediately flips back to positive. Your apology fixes the problem, making you look capable and effective in the process, and she appreciates you for it.

Scenario 3

Next, imagine that you can tell she feels bad when she complains, "Hey now, that's not right..." and you want to make her feel better. But you don't really understand her reaction or what you said that was so wrong, and you feel a little bit ashamed and self-critical for not being perfectly on top of things. Forgetting that you could just ask, you blame yourself for not being able to figure out her inner perspective. You want to put together an other-centered apology, but the only plan you can come up with is to say you're sorry, put yourself down, tell her that you love her, say something nice about her, and beg her forgiveness. Here's what you say:

- "I'm sorry! I guess I said the wrong thing. What a dummy I am sometimes! I love you so much. You are so wonderful. Won't you please forgive me?"

Instead of staying strong and feeling good about yourself, this response has you sounding weak and groveling. Your attempt to apologize may be founded on good intentions, and you included a positive Other focus, so she may give you a couple of points for that. But you've apologized without knowing exactly what you said that offended her, which makes you look weak. Also, you've tried to help her feel better at the expense of your dignity by awkwardly putting yourself down. Telling her that you love her and that she's wonderful are general statements that aren't really linked logically to the rest of the apology. Finally, in requesting forgiveness, you sound as though you're asking her to rescue you from feeling bad about yourself, which undermines your ability to rescue her from her bad feelings.

Now you have a new problem: she sees you as nice but weak. She has to wonder whether she should mother you back to self-confidence or whether you might be someone she could fool and take advantage of.

Scenario 4

Finally, imagine that you can tell she feels bad when she says, "Hey now, that's not right..." but you think the problem is that she's just too sensitive. You have no regrets about what you said and feel she should accept you exactly as you are and just deal with it. Not only do you not really understand her reaction or what you said that was wrong, but you also feel so extremely confident about yourself that you discount the possibility of having said anything wrong.

However, you know she feels bad and you want to sound like a gentleman and make her feel better so that you can look good and get on with your life. Thinking that using an other-centered apology is your ticket to making her feel better, here's what you say:

- "Is there something wrong with me giving my honest opinion about milk? [I feel insulted because I love milk.] I'm sorry, my dear! I didn't mean to insult you! I should have kept my thoughts to myself. I know how emotional you get about some things."

You begin by asking a question to gather information, but your question is Self-focused (Is there something wrong with me giving my honest opinion...) rather than mostly other-focused (You seem upset. Did my opinion of milk offend you?). Next, you apologize for insulting her, and you did that well enough. However, in trying to explain what you did wrong and then end with a positive Other focus, you said you should have kept your opinion of milk to yourself because she is so emotional! This implies that you think she's weak and incapable of handling the truth – making it a *negative* Other focus.

Overall, either of two problems can sabotage your efforts to give an other-centered apology: your lack of confidence and self-acceptance, or your overconfidence and lack of real regret.

Yet done effectively, the other-centered approach offers you an opportunity to make your woman feel better, get real closure on the issue, and not have to compromise away your honest opinion in the process. It leaves both of you feeling better about yourselves and one another.

A Topic-centered Approach

If you focus on how true or false a statement is, or on what is factually true about a topic from a relatively objective standpoint, you're using a topic-centered approach. A topic-centered approach is generally Topic focused or opinion focused, where the opinions are supported by facts.

Few people might guess that a dry, factual debate over the value of milk would be a good way of ending the discussion in our example. Still, some people use a topic-centered approach to a problematic conversation because they believe they can reduce or avoid bad feelings by sticking with logical reasoning.

Underneath this logical approach, people usually feel that if their position on the topic proves to be true and right, they'll win the debate – and winning will make them feel good (thus flipping their Self value from negative to positive on their Focus Triangles). By the same token, the person who loses the debate will probably end up feeling bad. Nevertheless, many people work hard in their conversations to be right and win the argument, thus proving their positive value by virtue of their superior intelligence (at least in their imaginations). This strategy is similar to the directly self-centered approach: beneath the surface, it's a win-lose proposition because it makes the Self go positive only by making the other person's Self go negative. The more logical and fact based the discussion is, the further removed it is from the direct offensiveness of a self-centered conversational approach – but also, the more hidden and repressed both people's emotions can become.

A topic-centered approach is ideal for discussions in many environments, such as the workplace or the classroom. However, to use a topic-centered approach at this point in your conversation, you both would have to become very objective and ignore the emotional side of the relationship.

In our example, you've already begun by giving your personal opinion of milk: "...for *babies*. Yuck." Next, your woman moved to a Topic focus, but only as a means of supporting her ultimate Self focus: "...Lots of people drink milk and really like it – including me!" To switch to a topic-centered approach, you might say:

- "Well, it's true that a lot of people love milk, but it's equally true that a lot of people hate milk. I just think that it's objectively bad for human beings to drink cow's milk, at least after a certain age. You should really read up on it and try soy milk or rice milk instead."

Now that you've set up a rational discussion, there's no apology in sight. Unfortunately, there's no resolution in sight, either. Your remarks imply that your opinion of milk has more logical support than hers. She may be tempted to debate you logically, try to swallow her feelings and learn from you, or just drop the issue. However, on some level your Topic focus feels to her like another insult because, as mentioned previously, her identity is closely linked to her perceptions of milk. Even if she tries to respond to you objectively, there'll be a price to pay in your relationship. Maybe the next time you talk about something *you* love, she'll have an objective argument about why *it's* bad. Or maybe she'll find other ways to criticize you logically in return for your milk insult.

In short, when something goes wrong in a relationship that calls for you to apologize, using a strictly Topic-focused response instead of an apology may help you feel strong and intelligent at the time, but it may not serve your best interests in the relationship.

Conversational Preferences

Generally, people show a preference for one of the three conversational focuses. Some people prefer to talk mostly about themselves and their experiences; these people have a lot of Self-focused "me-me-me" conversations as a way of getting the attention they seek and sharing their experiences and thoughts with others. Others prefer to keep conversations as objective as possible and hold rational, fact-based conversations more often than not, preferring to rely on a Topic focus at least partly as a way of keeping the conversation safely impersonal. Still others are socially oriented and have a preference for the Other focus, which means they like to ask questions and gather information about others rather than talking much about themselves, since intelligence gathering allows them to achieve their own private or professional objectives – including winning friends, influencing people, analyzing people, making sales, or getting votes.

Each conversational focus preference has its pros and cons. People who love to share their personal experiences and observations with others can be perceived as warm and friendly, open, honest, intimate, and emotionally authentic. Yet they may also be seen as self-centered, self-impressed, small-minded, boring chatterboxes. Those who love to think and talk objectively and logically about things may be perceived as intelligent and knowledgeable, interesting and thought provoking, worldly and high-minded, but they might also be seen as uncool, impersonal, weird, nerdy social misfits. And those who prefer using an Other focus to gather information about the people they meet might be viewed as friendly and outgoing, popular, interesting, socially sophisticated, and attractive, or on the other hand, as calculating, dishonest, manipulative frauds.

In short, no single conversational focus is superior to the others from a moral or ethical standpoint. Each focus can be used in a beneficial way and has an important place in your conversational repertoire. The superior conversationalist is the person who becomes equally comfortable using all three focuses and who seeks the optimal conversational focus at each juncture in a conversation.

As a rule of thumb, when something in your conversation isn't working, you can always try switching your conversational focus to see if it improves your conversational flow and gives you more satisfying results. This simple technique is not a panacea, but at times it can help you get along better with others.

By listening to yourself and to your woman over time, you may be able to determine your respective conversational focus preferences. Knowing that, you might want to try switching your focus at times for the purpose of potentially reducing conflict and gaining insight. This could result in fewer clashes between the two of you – clashes that might later require apologies.

This chapter has shown you the importance of understanding and sharing perspectives as well as focusing your attention effectively in conversations, particularly when you deliver an apology. In general, two of the most basic reasons many apologies fall short of maximum success are: 1) a failure to effectively utilize an other-centered approach, and 2) a failure to end the apology with a relevant, positive Other-focused statement or question.

In Chapter 3, you'll learn about the larger process that effective apologies serve. You'll also learn about how to time apologies to increase their effectiveness.

3

APOLOGIES IN THE BIG PICTURE

Search the Internet on the subject of how to apologize and you'll find many opinions. Some articles, many apparently written by women or by men attuned to women's needs, suggest that a man should be mindful of certain requirements when offering an acceptable and proper apology to a woman. Other articles, clearly written by men, advise *against* apologizing to a woman. They reason that apologizing shows weakness and undercuts a man's animal magnetism, prowess, and sex appeal.

The Internet Web site SoSuave.com offers examples of this second kind of opinion. A contributor on that site who calls himself "DeepBlue" writes:

> What happens when you apologize to a woman? She will give you massive approval, she will smile and think you're adorable, she will want to cuddle you like you're her little baby.
>
> In other words, you will start seeming LESS like somebody she'd want to screw.
>
> Generally a woman is sexually drawn to men who seem kind of like her dad – her first and most powerful image of manhood. And how often do Dads apologize to their kids for anything?
>
> If you feel that you must apologize to a woman, do so very, very sparingly.[7]

From a woman's viewpoint, DeepBlue's advice lacks integrity, since women feel that those who refuse to apologize whenever they owe it are being unfair and refusing to play by the rules. Yet DeepBlue brings up an important point: to most women, a man is less sexually attractive when he needs nurturing than when he appears strong and confident.

What do you think about this? Do decent, intelligent men with the integrity to apologize when appropriate really turn women off? Can't men who apologize when appropriate still project a powerful image? Or, are the decent men all a bunch of wimps on account of their integrity? And, are men who never say they're sorry really such masculine legends in their time? Or, are they mostly legends in their minds?

EFFECTIVE APOLOGIES BEGIN AND END WITH POWER

A person must possess himself and have a deep sense of security in fundamental principles and values in order to genuinely apologize.

– Stephen R. Covey[8]

If an effective apology makes you sound powerful, not powerless, where does that power come from? You begin with the power of free choice – the choice to deliver an apology at any given time or not. Three different schools of thought on this issue are the keep-the-peace philosophy, the top-dog philosophy, and the win-win philosophy.

The keep-the-peace philosophy says that when something in the relationship goes wrong and your woman expects or demands an apology, you should apologize to keep the peace in your relationship. Maybe you don't always want to apologize, and maybe plenty of times you think you shouldn't have to because you didn't really do anything wrong. But no matter. From a pragmatic standpoint, this philosophy says it's in your best interest to apologize when she demands it because, if you didn't apologize, she'd make your life miserable. Caving in is, by this logic, a compromise a man has to make to be with a woman who respects herself. Maybe it stinks, but at least you have the sense that you're trying to be a good guy. Compromising is worth it according to this philosophy because it enables you to avoid an argument and maintain harmony in the relationship. Then, by the principle of give-and-take, you earn the right to ask for things *you* want in return. Of course you don't feel powerful when you're essentially obeying your woman, so to feel powerful again you need to quickly switch your focus to other things, such as money, career, or sports.

The top-dog philosophy says that when something in the relationship goes wrong, you have to stand strong, remain in control, and keep your woman in line. Otherwise, you'd lose your power and she'd walk all over you. If she wants and demands an apology for something you did, you should generally refuse because giving her that satisfaction would give *her* the upper hand. According to this line of thinking, whoever apologizes *loses* and becomes the underdog. If you are a top dog, your primary goal in a love relationship is to maintain your top-dog position as an integral part of your virility. In other words, you believe that if you lost your ability to control

51

her, you'd lose interest in her sexually. Therefore, you reason that guarding your top-dog status is in her best interest as well as yours.

Sometimes top dogs do occasionally apologize after making mistakes that are obvious to others. But according to this philosophy, if you're a top dog, you feel that most of the time it's in your best interest to hide your guilt and put up a strong front so that you can remain in control and make sure she obeys you. If she thinks your attitude stinks and she complains about it, so what? You can show your power all the more by reminding her how lost and broke she'd be without you, thus putting her in her place and making her suffer until she gets back in line behind you. Let's face it: either you cave in or she does. The top-dog philosophy only works when somebody is on the bottom – and you want to be sure *she's* the one on the bottom. You might look like a jerk, but you believe that's okay because it's what a man has to do to secure his position as the leader.

The win-win philosophy says that when something in the relationship goes wrong and you decide you owe an apology, you have both a responsibility to do the right thing by apologizing and an opportunity to make yourself look good by apologizing like a pro. Your goal is to become masterful by mastering challenging situations, not by being the master in a master-servant relationship. In any given situation, your decision to offer an apology or withhold it would be based on the principles you've freely chosen to follow, such as the principles of fair play, compassion, and maturity. In deciding whether to apologize or what to say, the question isn't whether to cave or not to cave – the question is how to stay on top in the *big* picture by acting like a strong positive leader that your woman will continue to admire. Your intent is neither to be strong at her expense nor to appease her anger at the expense of your dignity. Rather, you want to show your leadership qualities of self-discipline and self-mastery by standing up for what is fair and right – and that includes apologizing when you believe it's fair and right to do so.

The strategy behind the win-win philosophy is to gain respect and admiration as a leader by virtue of your wisdom and mastery of each situation. Your wisdom comes from obeying the principles you believe in. And during those times when she takes the lead to teach you something, you have the confidence to give her credit for being right when she's right. Meanwhile, you accept the opportunity to master the lesson at hand as quickly as possible. Rather than competing with her right then, you compete with yourself to become more masterful today than you were yesterday.

If the best way to master the situation is to offer an apology, then you want to deliver one that not only addresses the problem, but also leaves you sounding strong, self-confident, and sophisticated. When apologizing, you don't aim merely to win back her approval, but also to win her admiration. Making a mistake, while regrettable, would immediately be interpreted as a sudden opportunity to look good by handling the apology with style, since you view an apology as a vehicle for showing off your exceptional social skills and your character. On the other hand, if an apology doesn't feel right, your aim is to manage the conversation just as masterfully so that you can lead her – in a gentlemanly way – to realize that she made a mistake, and perhaps to apologize to you if appropriate. In that case, you want to sound like a wise teacher or sage that she will admire and thank, once you help her "see the light."

The Price of Power

Each philosophy brings men a certain type of power. But for each philosophy, there's a price to be paid.

The man who keeps the peace may keep his woman happy and get a lot of what he wants in his relationship, overall. But the ongoing price he pays is an occasional loss of dignity in having to apologize when he doesn't believe he owes it. In terms of apologizing, he's more of a follower than a leader. How powerful is that? There's nothing wrong with being a follower in some areas of life and a leader in others. That's part of interdependence. However, there *is* something wrong with following the lead of someone who tries to force you to bow down and say something you don't believe by threatening to make you miserable if you don't. In that case, *she's* behaving like a strong negative leader. To be truly powerful, a man ought to be able to stand up to *negative* leadership and lead the conversation to a more mutually satisfying conclusion.

The man who sees himself as top dog gets most or perhaps all the little things he wants in his relationship, but not necessarily the big things. In terms of leadership types, he's a strong negative leader to whatever extent he resorts to power plays and force to get his way. If he's with a self-respecting woman, then once she realizes that he looks down on her, she'll have enough self-regard to fight back and try to get even for being treated like a second-class citizen. Eventually, thanks to his strong negative leadership, the top dog who goes for high-spirited women will either leave behind a string of failed relationships or end up in a relationship filled with complaints, bickering, trickery, verbal abuse, or even fights that could involve physical violence. How powerful is that? To the extent that a man can get his way through these methods, it's clearly powerful. However, in the bigger picture, the top dog lacks the power to make this kind of woman happy. To be truly powerful, a man ought to have the power to persuade, negotiate, and reason with his woman so that, without being threatened, cornered, or coerced, she would generally *want* to give him what he wants because she's getting what she wants from him.

On the other hand, if a top dog prefers to go for a woman who doesn't complain, fight back, or get even, then she may be so lacking in a will of her own that, over time, she'll bore him in conversation and in bed. How powerful is that? To get what he wants in a relationship of this nature, his wish is her command – unless he wishes for an exciting relationship. By constantly soliciting her admiration and agreement, he can feel powerful without having to show any significant power. Listening to her would be like listening to his own echo. Of course, if he's infatuated with his own words, this might leave him feeling sufficiently fulfilled. It's powerful in a way, just as an adult feels physically powerful when controlling a young child, or as a professor feels intellectually powerful when teaching freshmen. However, it's a weak form of power, since very little power needs to be exerted to get his way every single time. To be truly powerful in a worldly way, a man ought to have the power to attract an exciting woman with a will of her own, win her over, and keep her happy.

Often, a man who adopts the top-dog philosophy doesn't want to settle for either an argumentative woman or an overly agreeable one. To exercise his power maximally, he may opt for the subservient wife and then cheat with a series of more high-spirited girlfriends who sooner or later grow frustrated. Or, he may opt for women who tolerate and humor him because he's paying for their sexual services. This brand of top dog leaves behind a string of hurt, angry, or calculating women while remaining with a wife whose enthusiasm for him is slowly crushed. He measures his power with women by the scorecard he keeps of the number of times he gets his way each day and the number of women he conquers or purchases in his lifetime.

How powerful is that? It's very powerful, but in a destructive sense. It's a type of power that some men admire but other men do not respect. And few women, including his long-suffering wife if he has one, are impressed by him in the long run unless they get a kick out of having a constant battle.

Many times, women try to maintain their dignity by feeling sorry for this kind of man. Some women look back with regret, wishing their relationship with such a man could have lasted longer, not fully comprehending their subservient role in his self-serving game. Others, who realize how they were used and manipulated, actively despise him or even seek revenge. And the women he pays for sex see him as a business transaction, someone *they* use to add to their scorecards as measured by their bank accounts. The power to use women to get his every wish fulfilled is powerful, but it's a win-lose kind of power, which means the top dog attracts one loser after another.

The top-dog philosophy, when applied to a relationship with a woman, is riddled with irony: although a man may use his top-dog power to make love to countless women, he can't make a single one of them actually love him. And when a man uses his top-dog power to get an overly agreeable woman to do whatever he commands, he soon stops feeling excited about her. She may cling to him like a shadow clings to a living body, but the more she agrees with whatever he says, the emptier and more boring her love feels to him. In the end, a top dog gets little honest appreciation, admiration, trust, or acceptance from any woman.

A man who embraces the win-win philosophy can get both an exciting relationship over the long term *and* the ability to become increasingly powerful over the years in the context of his relationship. In terms of leadership types, his is a strong positive leader who leads himself forward in life as well as leading his woman in many ways, while following her in areas where she knows better. He wins the chance to find and keep an exciting woman, grows more attractive over the years as he grows in personal wisdom, and increases his sense of dignity. *That's power.* However, he has to pay upfront the highest price of all: he has to be willing to grow continually, say goodbye to childish thinking, and commit to being an adult.

The price of basic personal growth is paid in the time and effort it takes to trade in old illusions for more realistic ways of valuing yourself. Deep reflection, soul searching, and personal honesty and integrity lead to developing self-discipline, responsibility, and acceptance of your limitations and the limitations of others. The process may involve reading, discussing personal issues, writing in a journal, praying or meditating, or just taking time out now and again to think things over in a deep way. It often begins with the guidance and discipline of effective parents or with emulating a good role model. Sometimes being confronted by an important person later in life or challenged by a difficult life event triggers personal growth as well.

To be an adult, a man trades in his childish ways for the ideals of manhood. No more trying to please everyone or remain his mother's or father's good little boy; he accepts occasional disapproval from his parents and others as the price he pays for being true to himself and his principles. No more looking for favored-son status; he chooses to be fair to his siblings and others. No more Superman or Master-of-the-Universe delusions; while still aiming to be masterful in a realistic way, he accepts himself as a limited human being, embraces his humanness, and recommits himself to meaningful goals. No more trying to get something for nothing; he chooses to pay a fair price beforehand for what he takes so that he won't have to worry about getting caught and paying a higher price later on. No more acting cowardly, and on the other hand no more taking utterly foolish risks; he takes meaningful, calculated risks and accepts the consequences. By being fair and honest, taking responsibility for his actions, and apologizing for his mistakes, he earns the right to lead.

How powerful is that? It's the power of high principles being channeled through the individual man. A strong positive leader who looks out for the best interests of others while pursuing his own ambitions is the kind of man most women only dream of.

In the real world, many men who are strong positive leaders in business or within their communities may do everything necessary to keep the peace in their private lives, or may rely primarily on power plays in their relationships with women. Your choice of relationship philosophy – or philosophies – may vary from one arena of your life to another.

Additionally, your philosophy of power with women might fall into more than one category. For example, you might apologize to your woman just to keep the peace one day, use a top-dog power play the next, and then the third day create a win-win solution to some problem that earns you her admiration. The important thing to recognize is that your woman's feelings for you will shift back and forth as a result of whatever philosophy you put into practice. So, you don't have to be perfect, but the more often you take a win-win approach, the better she'll begin to feel about you – and the happier she'll be to follow your lead.

The Younger Woman Strategy

Many men adopt the strategy of marrying a much younger woman. Beyond sexual attraction and factors unique to each couple, this is one way for men to ensure that they'll remain powerful in their relationship, either according to the win-win philosophy or the top-dog philosophy. Since such a man has considerably more experience, he may assume it will be easy to lead his young wife and maintain the power advantage in the relationship. The younger woman, bowing to experience, maturity, and wisdom, is usually happy to follow her husband's lead, at least at first.

Sadly, this strategy doesn't always end well, at least when the younger woman sees herself as an equal partner and not subservient. Most women who position themselves as equals develop fairly good relationship skills sooner or later. Even if a man has a head start of one or more decades, his younger wife will likely continue developing her relationship skills in relation to him, especially in any area where she isn't fully satisfied with the way he treats her. If he doesn't at least match her pace of relationship growth, she'll eventually outgrow him and flip the power dynamic in the relationship to her advantage. This isn't because she necessarily wants to gain power over him, but more likely because she considers herself to be better equipped to lead the relationship in a principled way.

Women often lament the tendency of men to go for younger women. What they may not understand is how critically important it is for men to feel powerful in their relationships. When a man doesn't feel powerful enough in his relationship with a woman, he will generally do whatever it takes to restore his feeling of power. This isn't a question of good men vs.

bad men; feeling powerful is a need for all men. But different men adopt different philosophies of power and naturally use the set of techniques for feeling powerful according to the philosophy they adopt.

Likewise, men often lament the tendency of women to take more power in the relationship over time. What they may not understand is how critically important it is for a woman to respect her man's leadership as a strong positive leader, one who is fair and who caters to her needs and wants as much as to his own. If she loses respect for his leadership because she finds him to be too self-centered at her expense or because she feels that her voice isn't being heard and respected, she'll feel abused and neglected and instinctively try to take control out of self-defense.

Some men are convinced that women want all the power in relationships. While many men rebel in reaction to this perception, some men cave in, thereby allowing their masculine spirit to be crushed. Either way, these men lose because neither rebellion nor caving in sets the stage for a satisfying relationship. Although some women (and men) are actually sociopaths and have extreme ways of exerting power in a relationship, the vast majority of hetero women enjoy being with powerful men and dream of a man who combines strong, confident power with genuine love, care, and concern for her experience. When these women end up dominating in a relationship, it's usually not out of a drive to take power, but rather a drive for self-defense against a man who has consistently used his power selfishly at her expense. On the other hand, some women dominate because they have a partner who, for whatever reason, refuses to take the lead.

Men who feel the highest levels of confidence in their personal power tend to feel powerful with a woman their own age or older as well as younger. By adopting a win-win philosophy, you'll enhance your personal power with your woman over time, regardless of your age difference.

Learning to apologize effectively will enable you to meet your relationship challenges with greater confidence. When you begin your apology with a sense of your power and value and then succeed in apologizing effectively, your power is enhanced by your success.

EFFECTIVE APOLOGIES ARE WELL-TIMED WITHIN A LARGER PROCESS

Apologies generally happen in the context of bad feelings of some type. If you make a mistake that hurts your woman's feelings, you may apologize hoping to make her feel better. If your mistake makes you feel embarrassed or mad at yourself for hurting her feelings or for making the mistake, you may apologize hoping that her acceptance and forgiveness, or that displaying your good manners, will make you feel better. If she blames you for something you didn't even know was wrong, you may apologize hoping to make her feel better so that you can then feel better when she stops blaming you. If you do something slightly awkward, like step on her toes, you may quickly apologize as a matter of good manners, but you do so to avoid bad feelings that might arise if you didn't apologize.

In general terms, the larger process that an apology serves is the process of converting bad feelings to good feelings in your relationship. Some apologies accomplish the whole process. Other apologies play a role in a longer interaction. The specific purpose of an effective apology in this process is to enable you to help your woman recover after you do something you regret that makes her feel bad.

The Focus Triangles that follow show this process of going from bad feelings all around to good feelings all around. On the left, you can see the beginning of the process, where you each feel bad (-) about yourselves *and* about each other. A conversation or non-verbal communication takes place, represented by the arrow in the center. On the right, you can see the final result of the process: you've worked out your differences and you again feel good (+) about yourselves and each other.

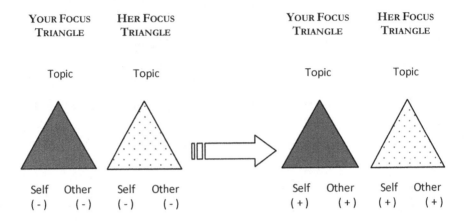

But here's the key: to be effective, an apology must be timed correctly within the larger process of converting bad feelings to good ones.

Before we get to the actual elements of an effective apology, it's important to understand the broader process of leading your woman and yourself from bad feelings to good feelings. This four-step process is the context that surrounds and includes an effective apology. Then we'll walk through an example.

Step 1: Flip Your View of Your Self to Positive

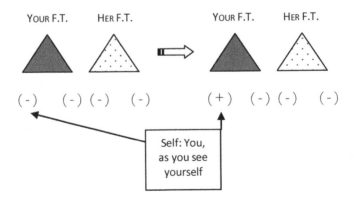

Men often make the mistake of offering an apology primarily to make themselves feel better after they've done something they regret. They reason that if their guilt dissipates through apologizing, then the apology will have served its purpose.

Although an effective apology does dissipate feelings of guilt, it's a mistake to apologize primarily to achieve this effect. That's because apologizing to your woman at a time when you feel lousy about yourself makes you look weak in her eyes, not powerful. Remember: an effective apology begins and ends with power. Offering an apology primarily to help yourself feel better could bring out her anger (because she would see your apology as self-serving), or it could bring out her inner nurturer (because she would see that you're in pain and feel sorry for you). Either way, you hand *her* the power to decide whether to help you feel better by forgiving you or not, and either way she will see you as weak. When she needs an apology from you, *she* feels weak (at least somewhere inside) and needs you to be strong to help her feel better again. If she sees you as weak, she might feel that you're trying to get her to take care of you rather than the other way around, and that would make her angry. She would then use the power advantage you've handed her against you.

That's why an apology is only truly effective when you already feel good (or good enough) about yourself before delivering it – not necessarily *overjoyed* about yourself, but self-accepting, self-forgiving, and honestly okay about yourself in spite of your mistake. By accepting yourself even though you made a mistake, you will then be able to speak your apology straight from your true center of power and provide her with the healing she needs. You'll sound confident and strong because you'll *be* confident and strong, not because you're a good actor trying to sound that way.

In other words, forgive yourself for your mistake in an honest way *before* you ask her to forgive you for it. After all, if it's reasonable to want her to forgive you for your mistake, then why shouldn't it be reasonable for you to think through your actions and intentions and forgive yourself first? If you can't forgive yourself for your mistake, why should she?

Step 2: Flip Your View of Her to Positive

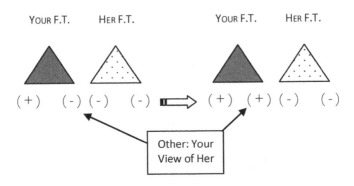

In addition to feeling good or okay about yourself, you also need a positive attitude toward your woman before your apology to her will be effective.

Why? If you offer an apology when you don't really see her in a positive light, your hidden resentment or negative judgment will very likely come across to her, even if you think you're covering it up. Because of the mixed message, your apology won't help her feel better, and she could easily think you're being insincere or downright dishonest. She may then feel justified in using your words against you in the future – or right at that very moment.

Also, why would you want to apologize to someone you don't see as good at the moment?

If your view of her is negative and judgmental at the time but, overall, you still care about her, begin by deciding that you *want* to see what's good about her in relation to the immediate situation. Then, open up a discussion (Step 3) with an initial goal of uncovering positive things about her in relation to the situation so that you can view her in a positive light.

Step 3: Lead a Discussion to Help Her Feel Better

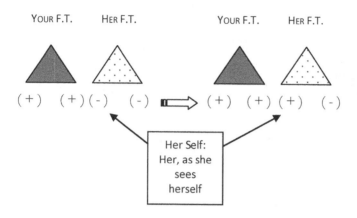

The main goal of this discussion should be to understand your woman's thoughts and feelings, share your positive intentions and honest perceptions (now that you feel better), and lead her to feel better about herself. If you don't initiate the discussion, she probably will in order to try to help herself feel better, but you can take the conversational lead by focusing on her and asking questions. You'll need to ask her about all the thoughts and feelings she's experiencing, and if appropriate, you may choose to apologize. Ask specific questions to gather information and use good listening skills and body language to focus your attention on her.

If you decide that an apology is called for, deliver it as soon as possible during the discussion – once you feel centered and care enough about her to want to help her feel better. In apologizing, the idea is to win her admiration by proving you're brave enough to own up to your mistake(s) and by proving to her that you care about her perspective and her feelings. As you learned in Chapter 2, end your apology with a positive Other focus to help complete the process of steering your relationship from bad feelings to good ones. Later, we'll go over more specifics about what the discussion and apology should include.

Step 4: Accept Her Appreciation and Follow Up

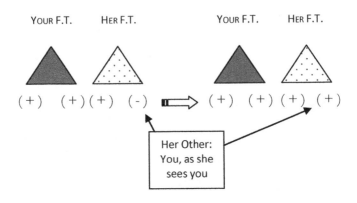

Once your discussion has helped your woman feel better, she'll automatically appreciate you. Her view of you will then flip from negative to positive without any further effort on your part, as long as she believes you were being sincere during the discussion. Follow-up is central to this process, as she won't feel good for long unless you follow your apology with appropriate action. For instance, if you apologized for making an offensive remark, be sure you don't make the same offensive remark to her in the future or she could use your apology against you. Lack of follow-up will undercut her healing process and reduce her ability to trust you.

An effective apology begins and ends with you feeling and being powerful. You begin with power by making the free choice to apologize – not because you have to, but because you choose to. Your bravery in owning up to your mistake will make you look psychologically or morally powerful from her perspective, and your success in making her feel better will immediately reinforce your sense of your own efficacy, another form of power.

When truly called for, an effective apology will help you feel better at the end than you felt at the beginning – but **not if rescuing your own value is your primary concern**. Apologizing will make you feel stronger and better only as a side-effect of helping her feel better, of being responsible and manly about it, and of turning a lousy situation into a better one.

Now, let's look at an example of how the whole process works.

YOU FORGOT YOUR ANNIVERSARY AND NOW SHE'S MAD

Some men would take the blame completely, and a lot of men would automatically apologize just as a matter of damage control, even if they didn't totally accept the blame. But let's say maybe you're not ready to do either. Maybe you thought that forgetting your anniversary wasn't totally your fault, since it's kind of unreasonable to be expected to remember these little things when you're busy with the important stuff, like working hard to bring in money. Don't sweat the small stuff, right?

You might have thought: "I work hard every day and that's what matters. She needs to grow up and get over it." If applying the keep-the-peace philosophy, you might think, "I'll recite the 'I'm sorry' line and go through the little ritual of *acting* like I'm sorry so that I can get this issue over with and we can both feel good again."

Whether you try to get her to grow up or whether you go through the ritual of saying you're sorry when you're only sorry that she's making a big deal out of it, she could *easily* use your words against you in the future.

Why? In the first place, she really can't grow up and dismiss her hurt feelings, since it's not a maturity issue for women. If you tried to convince her logically that she's immature for being so emotional, you might win the battle but lose the war. Her emotional nature is where her excitement for you lives; if she stopped being so emotional, her excitement for you would go flat. Rather, the issue for her is the basic human need to process emotions. As a man, you might process your emotions silently by thinking through them or taking some action. But as relationship expert John Gray explains in his landmark book, *Men are from Mars, Women are from Venus*, women usually process their stressful emotions differently.[9]

Most women can't process their hurt and anger very well without talking to someone about it (unless they quietly transform their feelings into cold revenge). Your woman could choose to talk to her friends about it, but her friends can't heal the pain for her. That's why she probably wants to talk out her thoughts and feelings with you and be reassured by your understanding and caring response to her. If her anger doesn't get processed, it's trouble, since her unprocessed anger will resurface later as strange moods or form an undercurrent of resentment, which she will definitely use against you in the future.

In the second place, if you act sorry without being sorry, eventually she'll probably catch on to your game. The moment that happens, her passionate feelings for you will diminish. Then, even if you tell yourself that she's the one who's off-base, you'll be the one losing out on her emotional gifts. And once you lose them, it's hard to earn them back.

In this case, you *know* you made a mistake in forgetting your anniversary, but you feel an inner resistance to apologizing.

When she informed you (in a disappointed and angry tone of voice) that you forgot your anniversary, here's what you said out loud to each other:

> YOU: I do 50 things right and one thing wrong, and all you do is yell at me about the one thing I do wrong!

> SHE: I know you do a lot of things right, honey. But it's our anniversary! I just can't believe you forgot! Apparently it doesn't mean that much to *you*.

On the following page are your respective Focus Triangles based on the thinking that follows your conversation at this point. The comments shown beneath the Self and Other labels represent hidden inner perspectives – things that each of you *feels and thinks* without necessarily *saying them out loud*.

Topic
[Forgotten anniversary (-)]

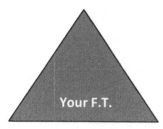

Your F.T.

Topic
[Forgotten anniversary (-)]

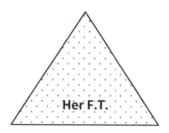

Her F.T.

Self [You (+/-)]	Other [Her (-)]	Self [Her (-)]	Other [You (+/-)]
I do 50 things right and one thing wrong, but I only get noticed for my goof. I think I'm darned good, so why doesn't she give me more credit?	She's not fair to me – doesn't give me enough credit for all the great things I do. Her behavior isn't very loving. Why doesn't she realize how lucky she is to be with me?	I feel like I'm last on his list of priorities. That hurts. Maybe I'm not attractive enough or smart enough. Maybe he's got someone else. I try to give him a lot but sometimes I feel used up. I'm tired!	He does a lot and he's really great, and maybe he's preoccupied with work, but he's just too self-centered. At work he gets a lot of glory, but then he comes home and soaks up my attention too. He's all about himself and doesn't give me enough attention in return for the attention I give him.

As you see above, you both view *you* as a mix of good and bad, and you both view *her* as simply bad, at least for the moment. You're not aware of what she's thinking, but you can see that she's really mad – and yet you're mad, too.

To prepare the way for leading your relationship back to good feelings all around, you need to see first yourself, then her, in a positive light, even if she doesn't. Then, if you decide to apologize for your mistake, you'll be in a position to do it successfully.

67

Understanding the Terrain of the Negative Self

Right now you're at odds. You might think it would be a good time to get it over with and say you're sorry so you can feel better. Unfortunately, she would probably feel worse, because she, too, would be in need of attention, and would think *you* should be paying immediate attention to *her* feelings and thoughts rather than going on about yourself and how sorry you are. By apologizing at this moment, you might be helping yourself feel better but you wouldn't be helping *her* feel better.

Whenever your Self goes negative, you automatically go into a state of inner crisis. It's often so brief and commonplace that you may not even notice it. This happens to everyone, regardless of gender. So to master effective apologies, you need to understand how this inner crisis works.

Inner Crisis Mode

When the Self goes negative on the Focus Triangle, the minus sign next to the Self signifies both negative thoughts about the Self *and* bad feelings (such as hurt, shame, or anger). That's because your thoughts can stimulate emotions, especially when those thoughts involve being judged as good or bad.

The bad thoughts and feelings, whether mild or intense, spark an inner crisis, because the very suggestion that you're not good is naturally upsetting and triggers an urgent need to act in order to erase or reverse it. Many people don't even notice this inner crisis state because it's so commonplace and because they react so instinctively to get themselves out of it. The term *Inner Crisis Mode (ICM)* is used here as a shorthand phrase (and acronym) to describe this experience of thought + feeling + urge for corrective action, which is a natural human response to the Self gone negative.

In any crisis, you need to take action. In ICM, you feel the need to *do something right away* to make your Self go positive. Typical actions include:

- Logically arguing against the negative remark or insinuation
- Silently marginalizing the status or intelligence of the person who said it to try to discount her message
- Pretending not to hear or understand the insult or insinuation

68

- Admitting to the behavior you're accused of but denying that the behavior is bad, or that you're bad for behaving that way
- Bringing in a friend, family member, or group to stick up for you
- Pointing out or thinking about other reasons you're really a good person in spite of the bad thing about you that was mentioned or implied
- Ridiculing or mocking the comment
- Devaluing the speaker through name calling or verbal attack
- Disconnecting yourself from the conversation, physically or mentally, to reject the speaker and focus on your own value
- Generating self-righteous anger or rage and possibly committing violence to feel and display your power, in a desperate attempt to stand up for yourself, take charge of something, and attract sympathy

In a typical one-on-one conversation in which at least one person goes into ICM, the devalued person often tries to rescue his own value by using either the *See-Saw Strategy* or the *Self-Affirming Strategy*. In the See-Saw Strategy, each person assumes the "good me/bad you" position, and each person's sense of value goes up and down like a child on a see-saw as both take turns trying to feel superior while putting the other down. In the Self-Affirming Strategy, the person in crisis generally draws the focus of the conversation directly to himself and asserts the "good me" position, sticking up for his positive value without stating any "bad you" out loud. Both strategies are problematic.

The See-Saw Strategy

> YOU: I do 50 things right (good me) and one thing wrong, (bad me) and all you do is yell at me about the one thing I do wrong! (bad you) You're not being fair. (bad you)

> SHE: I know you do a lot of things right, honey. (good you) But wait a minute! *I'm* not being fair to *you?* (bad me?) You know, I do a lot of things right, too, (good me) that you don't bother to even notice. (bad you) And yet I never forget the events that are important to you! (good me) I can't believe you forgot our anniversary, (bad you) and you haven't even apologized! (bad you)

69

YOU: Okay, I'm sorry. I know it's our anniversary. I just forgot, (bad me) *all right??* Jeez! (bad you) Sometimes I don't think you appreciate how hard I work just to give you a good life. (bad you, good me) You want me to give you romance, but that's unreasonable when I'm so busy. (bad you, good me) You need to stop being so self-centered and start appreciating all that I do for you rather than focusing on what I don't do. (bad you, good me)

SHE: *I'm* self-centered? (bad me?) You jerk! (bad you)

The above example shows you and your woman arguing with each other, each of you elevating your value and devaluing the other in an effort to feel better about yourselves. As you can see, the apology used was ineffective since it was calculated to make you look good, not to help her feel better. It's the kind of apology she may remind you of in the future and use against you because it contains hostility, rendering your apology insincere-sounding, which to her makes you appear lacking in personal integrity.

The See-Saw Strategy creates a conversational stalemate that leaves everybody feeling bad and mad. It's driven by the urgency of wanting to get out of ICM, but without a plan for getting you *both* out. Any time you're willing to push her down into an inner crisis in order to catapult yourself out of one, you can expect her to reciprocate. However, if you suddenly recognize that you're both in ICM, you may be able to step back and stop the madness long enough to refocus your conversation on the positive desires that lie beneath the negative feelings. In this example, the positive desires would be: 1) your desire to be appreciated for all the good things you do; 2) her desire for your attention, care, and respect toward her feelings and romantic needs; and 3) your mutual desire for fair play.

A variation of this strategy, the Logical See-Saw Strategy, happens when the argument becomes all about who's right and who's wrong. When an apology-related conversation is turned into a logical and impersonal (Topic focused) discussion, the person who ends up being right feels victorious or superior and therefore good. However, the person who is proven wrong feels defeated or inferior and therefore bad. For example:

YOU: I do 50 things right and one thing wrong, and all you do is yell at me about the one thing I do wrong! (That's a fact I'm right about.)

SHE: I know you do a lot of things right, honey. But actually I do give you credit for things. (You're wrong.) Why, just this morning I noticed how nice your tie looked, remember? (That proves you're wrong.)

YOU: No. You may have noticed my tie, but I don't recall you saying anything to me out loud about it. Maybe you just thought it. (You're wrong.) Anyway, I'm not talking about that, I'm talking about the important things I do – like how hard I work. As soon as I get home, all you can do is talk about yourself. (That proves you *don't* give me enough attention for all I do right.)

SHE: First of all, I did too say something this morning about how nice your tie looked. (I'm right and you're wrong.) Second of all, I always ask you how your day went. Don't blame me if you don't want to talk about it when I ask you. (You're wrong.) And I do not always talk about myself! (You're wrong about that, too.) Remember last week when you came home and went straight to the computer to play solitaire for half an hour even though it was dinnertime? And I didn't say a word! (See? That proves you're wrong.)

This Logical See-Saw conversation will probably end with an apparent winner and loser based on whoever was "proven" right. But regardless of who wins the argument, no one would end up happy because your deeper desires would remain unfulfilled: your desires to be acknowledged by each other, not just by yourselves, for your basic value and viewpoints; to get credit from each other for your good deeds; and to give and get romantic or loving attention in a way that satisfies both of you. In addition, the issues of forgetting your anniversary and the hurt it caused your woman have been sidelined and still need to be addressed and resolved.

The Self-Affirming Strategy

The Self-Affirming Strategy is another impulsive strategy that people use to try to rescue themselves from ICM. It is somewhat gentler than the See-Saw Strategy. Instead of playing a game of good & bad or right & wrong, this strategy plays a constant refrain of "me-me-me."

Of course, self-promotion is appropriate in many situations. But in a personal discussion of this nature, it can turn into a competition of who's better and whose needs are more important.

> YOU: I do 50 things right and one thing wrong, and I really wish I could get noticed more often for the things I do right! I think I deserve that much, don't I?

> SHE: Of course you do! And yes, you do lots of things right. But I have needs too. It's our anniversary, after all. Women don't take things like that lightly, you know. I got myself fixed up because I thought you were going to surprise me with an anniversary dinner or something. You know how important it is to me, and I don't really ask for that much, do I?

> YOU: Well, no, you don't. But you know that I've been super busy trying to make this deal go through. I'm really exhausted. And you know how important my paycheck is to both of us. I need some down time to relax tonight and that's all there is to it. I deserve that, don't I?

> SHE: Yes, you deserve a lot, but I do too, don't I? Today is our anniversary. I'm your wife, I'm ready to go out, and I deserve better than to be brushed aside like an afterthought on my own anniversary.

This strategy is not as openly hostile as the See-Saw Strategy. However, it's a tense discussion where each of you is trying to get your way via self-promotion. One partner will win and the other partner will give up.

No matter who wins, though, neither will feel truly satisfied. Each of you has a clear desire to be appreciated and celebrated by the other for the value and contributions you bring to the relationship. Because you both spend so much time appreciating and celebrating *yourselves* in this conversation, though, you both may lose any opportunity to receive that appreciation and celebration from one another in a sincere and meaningful way.

Fortunately, a technique derived from the Self-Affirming Strategy can lead to a better outcome. The technique is self-affirming self-talk, and it's used to begin the four-step process of bringing the relationship from bad feelings to good ones.

Step 1: Getting to Positive Self

When the conversation first began, here's what you said to each other:

> YOU: I do 50 things right and one thing wrong, and all you do is yell at me about the one thing I do wrong!

> SHE: I know you do a lot of things right, honey. But it's our anniversary! I just can't believe you forgot! Apparently it doesn't mean that much to *you.*

You're now both in ICM: you need immediate positive attention before you'll be able to focus on anything other than yourself, but she needs immediate positive attention to be able to focus on anything other than herself.

Because you're having an inner crisis, you absolutely have to take care of restoring your own value first. However, to be a good leader under the circumstances, you need talk to yourself *silently* and refrain from sharing your self-promotional thoughts with her or asking for her buy-in *yet.* On the outside, she'll see you as being silent and restrained, gathering your thoughts momentarily rather than speaking impulsively. That's a strong look. On the inside, you're being Self-focused in order to give yourself the positive attention you need to feel good again.

What You Think to Yourself	What You're Doing Right
Yes, I did forget our anniversary,	Admitting your mistake
but it was only because I was so busy. That's not great but it's understandable.	Tracing your reasons for doing what you did so you can forgive yourself
I *am* good – just look at all the things I do right –	Finding evidence of positive Self value
and somewhere inside she knows it.	Assuming more evidence of positive Self value and evidence that she is good as well
My desire has always been to be good to her,	Identifying one of your key motivations in the relationship
and I can still be good to her by making things up to her now.	Expressing hope that you can still succeed
I'll apologize now and ask her out for a getaway weekend in a couple of weeks.	Taking responsibility and forming a plan to make amends

At this point, you might be wondering, "What's wrong with just sharing these statements with her out loud, so that she, too, can see how good I am? Wouldn't that save time?"

Well, just imagine you said these things out loud to her right then, at a time when, as you know, she was in ICM. She might go along and try to listen to you, but deep down inside she'd be screaming: "HEY, LADIES FIRST!" . . . incensed that you kept talking about yourself instead of *her*.

To repeat, **Inner Crisis Mode always makes people self-centered** – not because they're fundamentally low and selfish but because they have *no choice* but to deal with *their* inner crisis before they can think clearly.

Even if your mistake was innocent and your motivations were pure, by talking out loud about yourself and your own value right away you would make her feel frustrated at the very least. She might not be able to hear a word of it because of her urgent need for attention, and she may easily decide that your words sound like a bunch of excuses even when they're not. Because she's in ICM, she can't think clearly yet. All she can do in this state is to focus on herself until she feels good about herself again. Then she'll be able to hear you better. She needs your help – but you can't help her until you silently pull *yourself* out of ICM.

Right now, your silent self-affirming self-talk has altered some of your thoughts, as shown beneath your Focus Triangle:

<table>
<tr><td colspan="2">Topic
[Forgotten anniversary (-)]</td><td colspan="2">Topic
[Forgotten anniversary (-)]</td></tr>
<tr><td colspan="2"></td><td colspan="2">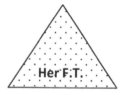</td></tr>
<tr><td>Self [You (+)]</td><td>Other [Her (-/+)]</td><td>Self [Her (-)]</td><td>Other [You (+/-)]</td></tr>
<tr><td>I made a mistake, but that's okay because I'm just human. I'm busy doing good things, I know I'm a good man, and I still want to be good to her – and now I've got a plan for making things up to her.</td><td>She's not fair to me – doesn't give me enough credit for all the great things I do. Her behavior isn't very loving. However, somewhere inside she knows I'm good, and that shows she's good too.</td><td>I feel like I'm last on his list of priorities. That hurts. Maybe I'm not attractive enough, or smart enough. Maybe he's got someone else. I try to give him a lot, but sometimes I feel used up. I'm tired!</td><td>He's really great, and maybe he's preoccupied with work, but he's just too self-centered. At work he gets a lot of glory, but then comes home and soaks up my attention too. He's all about himself and doesn't give me enough attention in return for the attention I give him.</td></tr>
</table>

Step 2: Getting to Positive Other

Now that you feel okay about yourself again, you think about her for a moment and realize that your accusation (that she only gives you attention for your missteps and not the things you do right) wasn't really fair. You see now that this was an exaggeration and that you only thought that way because you were in ICM. You realize that she didn't say or do anything unfair and that, in fact, she had every right to feel bad about being forgotten on your anniversary and to get mad about it.

Recognizing these things, you continue to adjust your thinking about her:

Topic	
[Forgotten anniversary (-)]	

Self [You (+)]	Other [Her (+/-)]
I made a mistake, but that's okay because I'm just human. I'm busy doing good things, I know I'm a good man, and I still want to be good to her – and now I've got a plan for making things up to her.	She's high maintenance, but she has a right to her anger and hurt because anniversaries mean a lot to women. She's a good woman and deep inside she knows I'm good. She wasn't really being unfair to me. She's just mad, frustrated, and disappointed.

Topic	
[Forgotten anniversary (-)]	

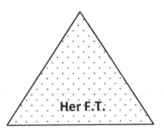

Self [Her (-)]	Other [You (+/-)]
I feel like I'm last on his list of priorities. That hurts. Maybe I'm not attractive enough, or smart enough. Maybe he's got someone else. I try to give him a lot, but sometimes I feel used up. I'm tired!	He does a lot and he's really great, and maybe he's preoccupied with work, but he's just too self-centered. At work he gets a lot of glory, but then he comes home and soaks up my attention too. He's all about himself and doesn't give me enough attention in return for the attention I give him.

At this stage in the process, you feel better about yourself and better about her. Therefore, it's time to move to Step 3.

Step 3: Leading the Discussion

After pausing to collect your thoughts, understand your actions and motivations, accept yourself as okay, and see her in a reasonably positive light, it's time to reopen the discussion.

Your main goal in leading the discussion is to help her see herself as good and as loved despite your mistake so that she can feel better again. To be her hero and healer, you'll rescue her from the inner crisis that your mistake has unintentionally created for her by interviewing her and leading her to reconnect with one of her key motivating desires for being in the relationship with you. Ultimately, you want to re-energize that key motivating desire.

To review, here is what you've said out loud to each other so far:

> YOU: I do 50 things right and one thing wrong, and all you do is yell at me about the one thing I do wrong!

> SHE: I know you do a lot of things right, honey. But it's our anniversary! I just can't believe you forgot! Apparently it doesn't mean that much to *you*.

When you started out with "I do 50 things right and one thing wrong . . .." you were sharing your inner perspective – your thoughts and frustrations – with her at a time when you were in ICM. Because ICM can distort a person's thinking, you made the mistake of falsely accusing her of not giving you enough attention for all that you do right.

After you paused, thought about your actions, and pulled yourself out of ICM, you realized that your assertion that she doesn't give you enough attention for all that you do right wasn't fair. You understand why you implied this, but now you realize that you have *two* reasons to apologize: 1) you forgot your anniversary, and 2) you falsely accused her of not giving you enough credit for all the things you do right.

To show your intention of helping her feel better, lead by owning up to your mistakes and sharing your new inner perspective in a caring, confident, and self-accepting way. Switch back and forth between a positive Self focus (where positive = honest and caring) and a positive Other focus.

> YOU: You're right, darling. I forgot, and I'm really sorry because I know it hurt your feelings. I've been super stressed about my projects at work. Even though I wrote our anniversary on my calendar, it slipped my mind. You do give me credit for doing things right. I guess I just felt frustrated at making such a stupid mistake and tried to make my forgetfulness partly your fault. It wasn't your fault, and I shouldn't have said that.

> SHE: I understand how much you do at work, and I appreciate it. But I have to say it felt really horrible to be forgotten on our anniversary.

Your apology has begun but is not yet complete. Before you can finish the process, you need to gather further information about her inner perspective. When she said, "...it felt really horrible to be forgotten" she was trying to share her inner perspective with you. The question is: has she shared everything she needs to share? Probably not, because her basic motivation for being in a relationship with you as it pertains to this situation isn't clear.

Women's vs. Men's Feeling-Related Talk

Generally, when a man feels bad, he may not say anything. He may withdraw, spend time alone, go into the basement or garage and think or get busy with something. If he says aloud, "I feel pretty bad," he may not feel the urge to elaborate.

But when a woman says, "I feel pretty bad," she may be revealing just the tip of the iceberg, hoping that her man will care enough to want to know much more about her thoughts and feelings. Women's feelings often go deep, and their minds are sometimes filled with ideas that you might never imagine. No matter how smart you are, you won't necessarily know all that she's thinking about or just how dramatically her bad feelings may be spiraling downward until you focus your attention on her and start asking questions to learn more.

If you don't inquire further, she may feel slighted. Although the conversation may come to a quicker ending that way, she would likely use her pent up thoughts and feelings against you in the future. But if you initiate and conduct a debriefing to find out all her related thoughts and feelings, with the idea in mind of rescuing her from her inner crisis, she'll feel loved because of all the attention you give her – even if her emotional outpouring sounds negative and insulting. When you debrief her by asking questions to find out all about her inner perspective in relation to the situation, it will feel to her like evidence that you care – provided you maintain a confident and compassionate attitude. She'll see the debriefing as a welcome dose of appropriate attention to her deeper thoughts and feelings, which are central to her identity and sense of value.

Good questions for getting to the heart of the matter may include:

- I can see that you feel bad, and I'm sorry about that because you're so good. Right now I'd like to understand your perspective more fully. Would you be willing to tell me more about how it felt to you?
- Do you have any more thoughts, feelings, fears or doubts to share with me about this situation?
- Is there anything else that's troubling you in regard to this incident? Are you sure?

These questions are not intended to be scripts; they're just meant as suggestions to give you the general idea. In any given situation, you have to use your judgment about what to ask and ask it in your own words. Your goal at this point is to learn as much as you can about her inner perspective and then show that you care by expressing compassion, personal concern, and sympathy. The conversation might go like this:

YOU: I can see that you still feel bad, and I'm truly sorry about that because you deserve better. Right now, I'd like to know more about how you felt when you realized I forgot our anniversary — and when I blamed you for not appreciating me enough. What did that feel like to you?

SHE: Well, I know you do a lot of good things, and I know you only implied that I don't notice all the things you do right because you were mad. But when I first realized that you forgot our anniversary, I felt really hurt. I thought maybe you don't care as much as you used to, or maybe I'm not so special to you anymore compared to all the talented men and women at your job.

YOU: I see. My forgetting our anniversary really brought up a lot of self-doubts, didn't it? I'm so sorry. I didn't mean to do that to you. Now I'm wondering what else you're thinking. Are there any other self-doubts you haven't mentioned yet?

SHE: Um, no. Well, okay. Then I started worrying that maybe there's someone else who means more to you. I guess I felt scared that maybe I'm a total fool and that you're tired of me. (She cries.)

Here's how your new conversation has affected your thinking and hers:

Topic
[Forgotten Anniversary (-)]

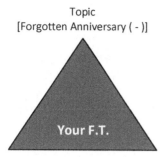

Your F.T.

Topic
[Forgotten Anniversary (-)]

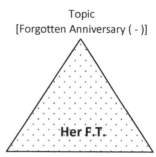

Her F.T.

Self [You (+/-)]	Other [Her (+)]	Self [Her (-/+)]	Other [You (+/-)]
I made a mistake, but that's okay because I'm just human. I'm busy doing good things, I know I'm a good man, and I still want to be good to her. Now I feel guilty for making her feel bad. But I've got a plan for making things up to her, so everything will be all right.	She's got such big feelings around the little things I do. Now I am starting to realize how powerful my influence is in her life. She must love me a lot to be willing to go through all these emotional ups and downs for me.	I feel hurt and angry and afraid that maybe I'm not so special to him anymore. But I also feel valuable because he cares enough to take the time to try to understand all my thoughts and feelings and to reassure me. I still want to be the woman of his dreams. Maybe somehow I can be.	He doesn't give me enough attention a lot of the time, and he made a really insulting mistake, but the attention he is giving me right now shows that he still cares.

At this point, she's shared enough of her inner perspective that you can identify one of the key desires that motivates her to be with you, along with the associated fear. Her relationship dream is to be special to you, the most special woman in your life. Her fear is that she isn't the most special woman in your life anymore, and that someone at work has replaced her in your mind and heart. At last, you have all the information you need so that you can resolve the whole situation by wrapping your apology around this key motivation.

YOU: You are such a sweetheart. You're the most special woman I've ever met. I'm amazed at how many bad feelings you're willing to go through on my account and yet still dream of being special to me. I know the timing is not perfect, but I would love to take you out for a getaway weekend in a couple of weeks so we can celebrate in style and I can give you the attention you deserve. My projects at work will be handled by then and we can have the whole weekend together, just the two of us. Would you like that, sweetie?

SHE: How can I resist? (She smiles.)

Step 4: Accepting Her Appreciation and Following Up

During your conversation, you reinforced your power in a manly way by being responsible, leading the conversation, and succeeding. In addition, you gave her much to appreciate and admire about you. Technically, you switched back and forth between focusing on yourself in positive ways and focusing on her in positive ways. When focusing on yourself, you owned up to both of your mistakes (showcasing your honesty and integrity), explained why they happened (showing her that it wasn't her fault), expressed regret for the harm your mistakes caused (showing that you care about her and not just yourself), and proposed a solution to make up for the first mistake (showing that you're responsible and good).

You don't feel good about making these mistakes, but you accept yourself and feel okay. You *do* feel good about the halo effect that comes with apologizing successfully. She now associates your words with maturity, responsibility, love, and integrity – qualities she desires in a leader.

When focusing on her, you listened to her with respect and concern as she shared her inner perspective. Next, you probed gently to find out what else was there. You recognized her value to you (willing to go through a lot of bad feelings and still desire you) and praised her for it. Finally, you uncovered her basic desire/fear (her dream of being special to you and her fear that she's not) and reaffirmed the dream for her in words and in proposed actions. Throughout the process you provided, and promised her more of, the most basic expression of love: appropriate attention.

Let's see how your Focus Triangles reflect each of your thinking at the end of this conversation.

Topic [Apology and proposal for getaway weekend (+)]

Topic [His apology and proposal for getaway weekend (+)]

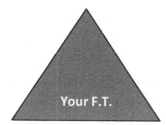

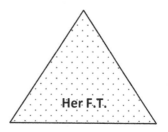

Self [You (+)]	Other [Her (+)]
I love her, I'm telling her I love her, and I'm proving it by spending a lot of time to help her feel better and by offering to make things up to her. Under the circumstances, I'm acting responsibly. I've earned the right to feel good about myself.	She's open to me even when I screw up. She's devoted to me and dreams of being special to me. She's a sweet woman.

Self [Her (+)]	Other [You (+)]
I want to be special to him, and he is listening to me patiently even though I'm upset. He is setting aside time to prove that I am special to him, and he promised to give me more time and attention soon. That makes me feel good.	He's very busy, but that's good because he makes good money. I'm so glad he wants to spend the time to understand and care and do whatever it takes to keep our love alive. I think he is being emotionally honest. He is a good man.

The more you give her appropriate attention thereafter, the better she'll feel about herself and about you. This doesn't necessarily mean you'd have to spend a lot more time with her. If you were busy with your career, you wouldn't have more time to give her. But even minutes a day of intense, appropriate attention to her thoughts and feelings (in place of half-hearted attention or excessive self-promotional talk) would help to ensure that neither the fact that you forgot your anniversary nor your apology for it would ever be used against you in the future . . . unless, of course, you failed to follow up by providing the getaway weekend you promised her, or unless you forgot your anniversary again in the future! If you were to fail to keep your promise, or if you should forget an anniversary in the future, it would only be because you didn't fully learn the lessons of this experience.

To be successful when apologizing, you have to do more than say the right words and make the right faces. You have to actually learn, understand, care, and remain open to discovering more about your woman and about yourself. And you have to prove your love by following through on your promises and avoiding the same mistakes in the future.

Strong positive leadership is rooted in character, and character springs from maturity. Strong positive leaders are people who are willing to accept being imperfect without beating themselves up for it. They mature by taking their mistakes in stride, being patient with themselves, and trying again until they get it right. Their strength comes not from being superhuman or being right all the time, but from being absolutely sure that it's okay and even good to be human, even though it means being flawed. These leaders know that the way to feel good about themselves is to accept themselves "warts and all," apologize with style when mistakes are made, and constantly strive to do better in a reasonable way, without getting overly stressed about it.

The paradox of maturity is that by admitting to your mistakes and embracing your humanness and limitations, you'll probably feel that you look bad. Yet from a woman's perspective, you'll acquire perhaps the most attractive trait of all: wisdom.

In this chapter you learned about different philosophies of power and their ramifications in your relationship. You also learned about the critical importance of feeling powerful when apologizing. You saw that an effective apology is a tool for helping to transform bad feelings in your relationship to good feelings after you've said or done something you regret, in a situation where your woman needs your help in recovering her value. It only works well after you've already forgiven yourself and seen your woman in a positive light. Any apology you offer that fails to serve the larger purpose of helping to transform bad feelings to good ones in your relationship is bound to be less than fully effective.

Knowing this, you're now ready for Chapter 4, where you'll read about specific elements of an effective apology.

4

APOLOGY ELEMENTS

A perfect script for apologizing in every situation does not exist. Simple apologies are useful for simple mistakes and multi-faceted apologies are better for serious offenses. In fact, there's no single correct way to apologize to a woman even for one particular mistake, such as forgetting an anniversary, since each relationship has a different history and since every woman is an individual with a unique set of sensibilities and personal preferences. The examples of apologies shown in this book will be more effective for some women than for others. However, by discovering your woman's apology preferences, you can position yourself for greater success in your current relationship.

In this chapter, you'll learn about several elements of an effective apology. Depending on the situation at any given time, you might want to use some or many of these elements when apologizing to your woman. You'll also learn what the women who participated in my 2010-11 Men's Apology Survey said about these apology elements. Finally, you'll see two extensive examples of apologies given under different circumstances: when the mistake you made was innocent and when it was not so innocent.

CONTENT OF AN APOLOGY

Many successful apologies are brief expressions of regret. If you literally stepped on your woman's toes, you wouldn't need to state, "I admit I've stepped on your toes," and you wouldn't need to explain why you did it, ask her to share her perspective on how it affected her, or reveal your plan for how to avoid making the same mistake in the future. You'd probably just say "oops" or "sorry" or express your regret through eye contact and a sympathetic facial expression.

On the other hand, an apology for infidelity would require all of the above elements and more, since without them your woman may not be able to get over her feelings of being betrayed and devalued.

What elements should your apology contain? Depending on the severity of your mistake or offense, so many different words and statements could be used. Sometimes you'll want to lead with owning up to your mistake, but at other times it may not be clear until late in the conversation that you've done or said anything that would require an apology.

Once you realize an apology is due and decide to provide it, you should consider not only what you think and feel about the situation, but also what matters most to your woman – what she needs to hear from you. In the book *The Five Languages of Apology: How to Experience Healing in All Your Relationships*, authors Gary Chapman and Jennifer Thomas introduce five key elements of an apology: "expressing regret, accepting responsibility, making restitution, genuinely repenting, and requesting forgiveness."[10] Furthermore, they say: "Husbands and wives typically do not have the same primary apology language. Consequently, their apologies are often met with resistance rather than forgiveness."[11] To help people learn more about these "languages of apology," Chapman and Thomas provide a simple self-test at the end of their book. Reading their book can help you learn more about apologizing in any relationship. In addition, if you both take the self-test, you may be able to identify which of these five elements you most need to use when apologizing to her – and which elements you might ask her to use when apologizing to *you*.

In this chapter, you'll see a longer list consisting of broad concepts for apologizing and specific apology elements for your consideration.

Men's Apology Survey

In August 2010 under the guidance of Dr. Andrea Burleson-Rutter, Ph.D., an organizational psychologist, I developed a Men's Apology Survey. Implemented online, this predominantly multiple-choice survey was designed to test the underlying assumptions of my book. I also hoped to gather further information from both men and women about their experiences, thoughts, and feelings on the subject and possibly uncover issues I had missed.

The survey was conducted from September 2010 through January 2011. All participants were anonymous volunteers, which means their responses do not necessarily reflect the opinions of a cross-section of society. Rather, survey results reflect the opinions of men and women who have an interest in the subject and a willingness to contribute their thoughts.

Participants were first asked the length (in years) of their longest hetero love relationship. Categories of 1–5, 6–15, 16–25, and 26+ years were about equally represented. Next, participants reported their gender. In total, 85 men and 85 women participated.

For men, the survey asked about: 1) attitudes toward apologizing to their woman, toward women's expectations regarding apologies, and toward power lost or gained when apologizing to their woman; 2) their emotional reactions as well as the emotional reactions of their woman during an apology; 3) their experiences when their apologies are accepted by their woman; 4) their experiences when their apologies are rejected by their woman; 5) the overall results of their apologies most of the time; 6) their experience of getting particularly positive results; and 7) a link between their ability to apologize effectively and their feelings of relationship competence.

For women, the survey asked about: 1) their man's willingness to apologize when they believe an apology is due; 2) the desirability of various apology elements; and 3) their typical feelings after an apology is received.

At the end of the survey, all participants were given an optional opportunity to sound off and say anything they wanted to say about the topic or about the survey. Full survey results are available at: http://howtoapologizetoyourwoman.com.

In general, the men's survey responses suggest that many men want to apologize effectively when they feel an apology is due. It also reflects many men's interest in learning an effective apology technique. Male participants disclosed a variety of experiences and opinions about the apology process throughout the survey and in their open-ended responses, which indicates that not all men experience apologizing in the same way.

Almost 80% of the men who took the survey saw apologizing as a self-enhancing activity. Specifically, male response frequencies to the question: "Do you feel that offering your woman an apology, when one is called for, makes you a better man?" were:

- Absolutely (49.4%)
- Probably (29.4%)
- Not sure (8.2%)
- Not much (9.4%)
- Absolutely not (3.5%)

In addition, more than 9 out of 10 male respondents indicated that learning an effective technique for apologizing would enhance their sense of relationship competence to some extent. Response frequencies to the survey question: "If you knew a technique for apologizing to your woman so effectively that you could make her feel better while being true to yourself every time, how much would this impact your feelings of competence in the relationship?" were:

- Totally (29.4%)
- Quite a bit (27.1%)
- Somewhat (25.9%)
- A little bit (9.4%)
- Not at all (8.2%)

The following page contains a chart showing the apology elements and concepts rated in the women's version of the Men's Apology Survey, ranked from highest to lowest. On the left is the ranking of each item's desirability according to the women who participated, along with raw score values shown in parentheses based on the actual survey responses. To the right of the apology items is a column you can use to take notes. You might want to use this list to open a discussion with your woman about her personal preferences. Or, you may prefer to check off things you'd like to try, just to see how they work for you.

As you can see, some apology elements at the bottom of the list are marked "unrated." These elements were not included in the survey, but they might be meaningful to some women. Also, if your woman thinks of an apology element not listed in this section that she'd like you to consider, there's room to write it at the bottom of the list.

RANK	APOLOGY ELEMENTS / BROAD CONCEPTS	NOTES
1 (369)	Speak honestly to your woman, even if it leads to further difficulties.	
2 (365)	Focus primarily on her feelings, needs, and desires during the apology and respond to them in a caring way, rather than focusing mostly on yourself and your mistake or offense.	
3 (353)	Ask for your woman's point of view and then listen to her respectfully.	
4 (335)	Do not make excuses.	
5 (334)	Begin taking clear steps to ensure that whatever you did won't happen again.	
6 (328)	Acknowledge the bad effects of your behavior on your woman (and on others, if applicable), and express regret for the harm you caused.	
7 (326)	Say you are sorry.	
8 (325)	Explain why you behaved as you did.	
9 (319)	Let your woman know that she did not deserve the pain and suffering you caused her.	
10 (314)	Own up: admit that you were wrong or mistaken.	
11 (310)	State exactly what you did or said that was wrong or mistaken.	
12 (293)	Share with your woman any insights you gained through the experience or any lessons you learned about yourself, about her, or about life.	
13 (260)	Make things up to her immediately, or propose an action plan for making things up to her.	
14 (234)	Ask for forgiveness.	
Unrated	Say "I apologize."	
Unrated	Say "I'm responsible" or "I take responsibility."	
Unrated	Say "It was my fault."	
Other:		

To recap: The rankings shown at the left of the chart are based on *averaged* responses of the female survey participants. Apology elements ranked highest (at the top) are things that most of the women taking the survey agreed were most desirable. If you plan to apologize to your woman but are unsure of her preferences, consider including items shown at the top of the chart. However, you don't have to *begin* with those elements or concepts, since that wouldn't make sense conversationally.

Beyond these survey statistics, it's important to recognize that your woman is not an *average woman!* She is a *special* woman with very particular sensitivities and personal preferences. The apology preferences of a few women who took this survey were strikingly different from the preferences of many of the other women who took the survey. Therefore, to position yourself for future success with your woman, take time to discover – whether through trial and error, casual discussion, a self-test (for her), or a structured interview – which apology elements are most meaningful to her and which ones she does not appreciate. Then use her feedback as a guideline, not a strict rule, since the kind of apology she needs from you at any point in time will still depend on the situation.

Interestingly, some traditional concepts of how to apologize include using the phrases "I was wrong" and "I'm sorry," and yet these apology elements are ranked 7th and 10th out of 14 elements by the women surveyed. Of course, the #1 most desirable element on this chart is to be honest, and it seems likely that many women would consider statements like "I was wrong" and "I'm sorry" to qualify as being honest. On the other hand, both "I was wrong" and "I'm sorry" begin with the word *I*, which means they're basically Self-focused, whereas women's second and third most desirable apology elements according to this survey involve focusing your apology on her and asking her to share her thoughts and feelings while you listen respectfully. These are both Other-focused. My interpretation: after saying "I was wrong" or "I'm sorry," switch to an Other focus.

Another curious result is that saying "sorry" (#7) is ranked a little lower than acknowledging and expressing regret for harm caused (#6). Of course, "I'm sorry" is an expression of regret, but unless a man states *what* he regrets or is sorry for, it seems that these women find the words "I'm sorry" a little less desirable.

A traditional concept among men for gaining closure after an apology is to give the woman flowers or a card. However, notice that the element: "Make things up to her immediately, or propose an action plan for making things up to her" falls 13th out of 14 elements. This doesn't mean that giving your woman flowers or a card is a bad idea, but it may mean that some women are more impressed by this kind of gesture than others.

If you decide to offer a tangible gift in an effort to gain closure, remember that a woman may respond differently to the same gesture under different circumstances. Your woman might absolutely love to receive a card or flowers, dinner and a show, or maybe some jewelry – occasionally. However, the same gift every time could get old. Depending on the situation, she might prefer to receive a concession on some point of contention, and a gift in lieu of a concession might be insulting to her. Or, if her upset has to do with an attitude of yours that she wants you to change, she might consider any gift you offer to be a game and possibly an attempt to silence her. Each woman has her own ideas about how her man should make things up to her in any given situation. That's why talking with your woman to learn about her thoughts and preferences might be a good idea, whether in a formal discussion or a casual conversation.

Apology Examples

Now we'll look at two examples of extensive apologies involving multiple elements, each offered to the same woman for the same mistake of forgetting an anniversary, but under different circumstances.

An Innocent Mistake

The chart on the following page illustrates important elements of an effective apology in a case where you forgot your anniversary but your mistake was a relatively innocent one. You'll remember this example from Chapter 3. Each element shown is designed not only to help flip her Self value to positive on her Focus Triangle, but also to make you look good by helping her do so, thus flipping her Other value to positive, too.

Elements of an Apology: An Innocent Mistake

APOLOGY ELEMENTS	EXAMPLE	FOCUS	FUNCTION
Own up to your mistake & express regret.	"Wow, I blew it. I can't believe I forgot our anniversary! I'm so sorry."	Self & Topic focus	Allows you to be honest, accept your humanness, and show you care
Without making excuses, explain why you think you made the mistake.	"I had it written on my calendar, but I've been so busy at work that I lost track. It wasn't intentional, honey."	Self & Topic focus	Gives her a way to understand that you're still a good person and that it wasn't her fault
Own up to the consequences of your actions, express your regret, and end your statement by focusing on her value.	"But I know that I've hurt your feelings, and I really regret it. I love you. You are good and you didn't deserve this."	Transition from Self to Other focus	Makes you look responsible, decent, and caring; allows her to feel valued
Ask her to tell you all about her inner perspective on how your words or actions hurt her; listen carefully; probe until she tells all (as if reopening the wound to clean out the infection); and express sympathy (as a first step in closing the wound).	"Please tell me how bad it feels so that I can understand the impact I've had." (Listen.) "I'm amazed at the emotions you have to go through as a woman. You poor thing. You deserve better than this."	Self to Other focus	Allows you to display your caring nature, learn about her key motivations for being with you, and find out how the event clashed with her dreams; allows her to get attention that helps her heal
Express your positive intentions; propose your plan for making things right based on reinforcing her key motivation for being in the relationship; end with a request for acceptance.	"I want to make it up to you. I know the timing is late, but would you like to go for a getaway weekend in two weeks? That'll give me a chance to show you just how special you are to me. Would you like that?"	Self, Topic, and Other focus	Allows you to bring good feelings back to your relationship; allows you to win back her appreciation, admiration, and trust

How does this apology make you look good? Owning up to your mistake makes you look courageous and honest, which helps her admire you again. Explaining why you think you made the mistake makes you look thoughtful and sincere. It also reassures her that it wasn't her fault and gives her a way to understand you so that she can like you again. Expressing honest regret about your mistake makes you look decent, and expressing regret for the harm or hurt you caused her by your mistake makes her feel cared for, which helps her heal. Focusing on her value makes you look unselfish and caring, while it makes her feel valued and valuable. Expressing your positive intentions may make you sound committed to being a good person, as long as she senses that you mean it. Asking her to share her inner perspective with you, and then listening sympathetically and probing further to be sure she's telling you everything she wants to say about it, makes you look exceptionally caring and committed to her – willing to pour a huge amount of appropriate attention into her personal concerns. That makes her feel truly loved. Proposing a plan for making things up to her demonstrates to her that you have integrity and helps her feel more fully satisfied with your response, as long as she trusts that you will follow through. Finally, asking her whether she will accept your proposal shows that you are courageous in giving her a choice, as well as respectful of her right to accept or reject your proposal, which makes her feel respected and important. The proposal itself, when implemented, helps to complete the healing process.

Of course, this apology would only be effective if you delivered it honestly and straight from the heart, not straight from some playbook – and only if your woman appreciated hearing these things said out loud.

A Not-So-Innocent Mistake

In some situations in which you feel you owe an apology, it may be difficult to stop the hurt you've caused. For instance, you might have said something rude that you honestly felt was true but that you were trying to keep to yourself, and it just slipped out. Or, you might actually have tried to inflict pain by insulting your woman in order to gain a power advantage, to avoid a topic that you felt was too humiliating to deal with, or to get even for something she recently said or did.

In situations like these, you have some work to do before you'll be ready to apologize. To move toward good feelings together, hold a discussion and explore your negative thoughts and feelings as well as hers. Eventually, when you can see both yourself and her in a better light, you can wrap up the bad-to-good feelings process through an effective apology.

For the sake of understanding how to apologize after you've said something intentionally hurtful, imagine this exchange:

> YOU: I do 50 things right and one thing wrong, and all you do is yell at me about the one thing I do wrong!

> SHE: I know you do a lot of things right, honey. But it's our anniversary! I just can't believe you forgot! Apparently it doesn't mean that much to *you*.

> YOU: Oh really? Well, maybe I forgot because *you're* such a *bitch*!

At this point, some anger has surfaced that may have partially driven you to forget your anniversary. There's not much you can say to take the pain away since, as far as she's concerned, you sounded as though you were giving your honest opinion when you called her a bitch.

You might think you could later say, "You're not *really* a bitch. I didn't mean it." But this comment is only effective if you can explain convincingly what caused you to say it when it wasn't true. Without a longer conversation to gain understanding, your back-peddling will probably make her question why she should trust your word this time when your word was the opposite just a moment prior. This could lead her to doubt your honesty in general.

Another typical way of handling this situation is to say something like: "Sorry I called you a bitch. I promise I'll never call you that again." This response isn't very effective, either. Sure, you might have every intention of not calling her a bad name ever again, but even if you don't, how will that help her feel better now? She still knows what you think of her, and such a negative opinion would still threaten her basic dream of being the beautiful, beloved, respected woman she always dreamed she would be.

At best, this response will make her feel wary of you. She may become vigilant for the rest of your relationship in an effort to ensure that you're being honest with her. If you ever again called her a bitch or other bad name, she would probably remind you of your promise and shame you for breaking it. In effect, by promising not to call her names in the future, you'd be assigning her the role of watchdog or enforcer in your relationship, which would not help her trust you or relax when she's with you.

Also, making a promise such as: "I promise I'll never call you that name again" is, in effect, shining positive attention on *yourself* by asking her for a favor – asking *her* to give *you* the benefit of the doubt. If you want to help her feel better, this is the wrong direction for your focus of attention to flow. Since an effective apology is a tool for helping you and your woman complete the process of getting back to good feelings, using a line like "I promise I'll never say that again" just doesn't work because she'll feel cheated out of the positive attention she should be getting from you. She needs you to help her heal from the wounds you inflicted by forgetting her on your anniversary, claiming that she doesn't give you enough credit, and then calling her a bitch. She doesn't need to play *mom* to you by reassuring you that you're okay and trustworthy, right after you've insulted her. In short, your words might make you feel better but they'll only make her feel worse.

The right way to handle this kind of apology is to have a long enough discussion to:

- ◆ Recognize and admit that you may have been motivated by negative or mixed feelings (while realizing that it's okay because you're human), and then emphasize your need to sort them out and get some clarity before continuing the discussion.
- ◆ Help her learn about you by stating your honest thoughts and feelings, including the negative ones, without apologizing for them (but without any name-calling or otherwise devaluing rhetoric), and then ask for her response so that you can learn more about her. Repeat this process and maintain a learning approach, not a blaming approach, until you understand each of your positive underlying motivations and recognize

which of your basic relationship motivations have been undercut and need to be revived.

+ End by telling your woman, in as much detail as possible, what you've learned or realized about yourself and about her as you complete any apology you see fit to offer.

Many women easily flip back and forth between playing a feminine role and playing a motherly role, sometimes without even realizing it. When you behave in a way that your woman perceives to be immature, she may automatically flip to her motherly role. By explaining to her what you've learned about yourself and about her, you'll help her feel that the trouble you've caused her has at least led to a positive outcome: you've matured. Then she'll be able to relax and return to playing the role of your woman instead of your mother.

The trick to apologizing effectively in this kind of situation is to use your conversation as a learning opportunity. She may or may not have a desire to hear you communicate out loud what you've learned, but she'll definitely want to know that you've gained a better, deeper understanding of her and of yourself. However, if you give her a "song and dance" about what you've learned while actually hanging on to your old attitudes, she'll eventually use your apology – and your continued immature, self-centered behavior – against you in the future with total justification.

On the following page you'll see another chart, this time showing additional apology elements. These additional elements are designed for times when you want to help her feel better after you've dealt her a not-so-innocent personal blow.

Elements of an Apology: A Not-So-Innocent Mistake

APOLOGY ELEMENTS	EXAMPLE	FOCUS	FUNCTION
After listening to her thoughts and feelings and realizing that you had mixed motivations, admit it with an air of self-acceptance, not self-righteousness. Then emphasize your desire to sort out your thoughts and feelings so you can make things right.	"I see now that I was trying to blame you for my mistake, and that was wrong. I'm sorry. But I'm afraid I have some mixed feelings about our relationship that might have motivated me to forget our anniversary. I need to sort out my thoughts. I love you and I want to work this out with you, but I need to postpone this conversation until later tonight. Maybe after dinner?"	Self, Topic and Other focus	Allows you to share your honest inner perspective, thus displaying your courage, integrity, and desire to make things right; allows her to gain insight and learn more about you
	----- Later -----		
Share your personal thoughts and feelings, including negative ones, in a self-controlled but firm way to help her learn about you; ask for her viewpoint and stay open to learning more from her.	YOU: "I've been feeling kind of neglected for a long time now. I think it started back when you got hooked on your cable TV shows and I started to feel like a third wheel. It felt like you suddenly started ignoring me. Do you remember that?" SHE: "Yes, I do. I never knew when you would be coming home at night, and I realized I could at least count on my TV shows to be there for me on schedule."	Self, Topic, and Other focus for both parties	Allows you to clear the air about your grievances and get the attention you want from her; enables you to take turns sharing your perspectives until you learn enough about each other to resolve your differences
If you've learned something new about her, or about yourself, tell her what you've learned; then complete any apology that makes sense and finish the process of getting back to good feelings together.	YOU: "Wow, I never realized what a bad effect my work schedule has on you. It makes sense, but I just didn't put it together before. Sometimes I forget how much you need me. I'm sorry I called you a bitch – you're not a bitch, you're a woman who feels lonely. How about if we carve out some special time now to focus on each other and plan a way to celebrate our anniversary in the near future?"	Self, Topic, and Other focus	Allows you to prove that you've understood her; helps her to relax and feel feminine again instead of motherly; ends the conversation with a plan to make things right

Again, the above examples are not intended as scripts. Some women will want to hear every element of your apology stated out loud. Others may appreciate some or most aspects of your apology to remain nonverbal, expressed only through facial expressions, body language, and especially actions. Being on the receiving end of your apologies, your woman is the best judge of what your apologies to her should and shouldn't include.

Fundamentally, you shouldn't have to apologize for being human, since you were made to be human and you're supposed to be human. If you accept being human as the right thing to be, it doesn't make any sense to feel bad that you're imperfect and that you sometimes make mistakes, even big ones. In fact, feeling excessively bad about such things will cause you unnecessary guilt, which triggers self-righteousness and self-absorption. These feelings will block you from being able to get outside yourself and turn your attention to others.

Even when your relationship is complicated and your intentions *are* to inflict harm, it's possible to reach back and look honestly at the respectable principle(s) that drove your bad intentions – the principle of justice, your masculine need to feel powerful in the relationship in certain key respects, or the desperate but universal need to make your Self go positive when you're in ICM.

After tracing your thoughts and actions back a few steps to uncover your more honorable thoughts, feelings, and desires, you can be honestly sorry about how far things seem to have gotten out of control, owning that your actions had something to do with it even if you don't yet fully understand how it all snowballed. With effort and the benefit of more successful strategies and techniques, you can learn to trace your motivations back far enough to see your own basic value, handle your respective inner crises in a more humane and effective way whenever you find yourselves there once again, and learn to get what you each want and need in more strategic and balanced ways.

Now that you know the basic components of an effective apology, you're ready to acquire some critical techniques for handling difficult emotions during the apology-related discussion. Chapters 5 and 6 provide ideas for how to handle overwhelming feelings – both yours and hers – like a strong positive leader.

5

HANDLING FEELINGS:
YOURS FIRST

What happens when you're stuck in Inner Crisis Mode and you can't seem to talk yourself down? Or blindsided in the midst of a conversation by an accusation or attitude that throws you into an inner crisis? Either way, recovering your cool can be a challenge.

PROTECT YOURSELF BY DEVELOPING WINNING SOLUTIONS

In the midst of a disagreement with your woman, you have two challenges: 1) resolving the disagreement, and 2) ensuring that neither the solution nor the way you get to the solution creates fallout.

For example, let's say you and your woman agree that you want to see a movie, but you want to see an action film and she wants to see a romantic comedy. Here are your challenges:

1. Choosing which movie to attend
2. Ensuring that neither of you ends up feeling bad about the choice or the way it was made

A winning solution that takes care of both challenges might be to agree on seeing both movies within the next week. However, if you decide to see the movie *you* want because, after all, you're paying, you could later be faced with your woman's resentment. Or, if you decide to see the movie *she* wants because you see how disappointed she'd be if you didn't, then you may be left with a lingering resentment.

Similarly, when giving an apology – one that won't be used against you in the future – you need to pay attention to the challenges of:

1. Deciding when to apologize and what to say
2. Ensuring that neither of you ends up feeling bad about your choice of apology or the way it was delivered

Imagine that you took her to the romantic comedy. She enjoyed it and you didn't. Afterwards you made a wisecrack about the film's main characters. You tried using lighthearted humor but it came out wrong. Then she called you a jerk. Now she's mad and expects you to apologize for being a jerk.

It just so happens that when you were young, your mother called you a "little jerk" so often that even now as an adult, just hearing the word *jerk* sends you straight into ICM. You think to yourself, "I gave up my evening to take her to this stupid romantic comedy, and now *I* have to apologize? I can't help it if the characters were lame. I'm in a no-win situation. If I apologize for what I said, I'll feel like puking. If I don't, she'll be mad at me."

You reason that it must be the wrong time to apologize since you don't feel good about yourself. In fact, you feel almost like a victim. You really don't see why you should have to apologize anyway – but you don't see another way out. What should you do?

Reconnect with Your Positive Motivations

When your mind is spinning around due to an inner crisis, it might seem impossible to silently sort out your thoughts and feelings and come out feeling good. You may need to talk – but how? To simply blurt out your bad and mad feelings would make you sound weak. She might respond by helping you in a motherly way or by arguing or lecturing you in an effort to teach you a lesson. Apologizing when you don't mean it is no solution either. That would degrade the value of your word and leave you with a bad taste in your mouth. And, given that such an apology would be dishonest, she might not believe it anyway, thus tarnishing your credibility.

Whether you call a time-out and walk away for a few minutes or try to address the situation and think on your feet, your challenge is to first reconnect with your positive motivations. Sort through your basic good intentions until you find the positive desires that drove your behavior, such as your desire to be emotionally honest with her when talking about the movie. Think about your positive motivations in your relationship, such as your desire to be a good man, which led you to take her to the movie she wanted to see. These thoughts will help to restore your confidence and make it easier to speak to her in a rational way.

But keep in mind that this isn't the time to convince your woman of how good you are, since she's in ICM too. Only helping her out of ICM will convince her of that. Instead, explain why you did what you did by identifying your positive intentions. Show self-confidence, not defensiveness. Granted, she may feel antagonized by hearing you talk about anyone else but her. However, once you state your basic positive intentions confidently, you'll be ready to try to see her in a positive light. Next, follow the techniques you've learned: shower her with lots of appropriate attention by listening to her, ask her to tell you more, and identify her key motivation(s) for being in a relationship with you. Your goal, after you get a clue about what dream of hers has been threatened or shattered (in her view) by your behavior, will be to reinforce her belief that her dream can still come true. This may or may not involve providing an apology. You'll figure that out as the conversation progresses.

Here's what you might say:

> YOU: When I agreed to take you to the romantic comedy instead of the action movie I wanted to see, I did it because I wanted to make you happy. I wanted to show that I cared. (Now you feel confident and can start focusing on her in a positive way.)

> SHE: Okay, but you didn't have to be such a jerk about it. If you wanted to make me happy, then why make me feel bad afterwards about what I enjoy? You give me something I want, and then you insult me for it. Nice! (She's still in ICM and can't think about your viewpoint.)

> YOU: (Ignoring the *jerk* comment because you can see that she's in ICM) Listen, I'm sorry I made you feel bad. I can see that I hurt your feelings and I didn't mean to. (Here you've apologized for the negative effects of your wisecrack, but not for being a jerk.) But help me understand: just how bad did it feel to you when I made fun of those characters?

> SHE: Very bad! It felt like you think romantic love is stupid and sappy and not real. What does that say about you and me? Do you think my need for romance is stupid, too? Maybe that's why you're not very romantic with me. Maybe you don't really love me at all — maybe you think *I'm* stupid. Maybe you think all women are stupid! (She's still in ICM but she has revealed her fears and key motivations.)

YOU: Wow, I didn't realize that I was making you feel unloved, or that you felt I was ridiculing your intelligence! You're a beautiful woman, and all women dream of romantic love. Of course there's nothing stupid about being a woman and wanting what women want. Women are great, and romance is part of your nature. You have a beautiful, feminine nature. I love your nature.

SHE: Really?

YOU: I guess I'm not the world's most romantic guy, but I really do love you – more than those movie stars ever could. Maybe I resented how happy those corny characters seemed, or how things always work out so well for *them*, or how you seemed to drool over that lead character, what's-his-name.

SHE: Ha ha, you're jealous!

YOU: Okay, maybe I'm a little jealous, but hey, I'll get over it. Anyway, romance always seemed kind of phony to me. But obviously, some women get romanced, so by comparison, I can kind of see how you might feel cheated when you don't get it too. You don't deserve to be cheated – you deserve the best.

SHE: Thank you.

YOU: So if my taking you to see a romantic comedy once in a while helps you reconnect with your romantic feelings, and if that helps you feel more loved, I can appreciate that. I want to do that for you.

Don't Take It Personally When She's in ICM

What you did right in the above example was to lead the conversation with confidence, recognize that she was in ICM, and refuse to take her "jerk" comment personally the second time around. You saw that her "jerk" comment was a reflection of her pain, not a true description of you. Instead, you sloughed off her insult, apologized for hurting her feelings, and began to explore the *depth* of her feelings. You listened well and responded sympathetically until you identified and understood her key motivations: getting romantic attention from you as a form of love, and being respected for her womanly desire for it. Also, you saw the dream connected to it – her dream of being the truly loved, valued woman she always hoped she would be.

Below is another version of the same scenario. This time, instead of handling the situation with confidence, you slip back into ICM after she called you a "jerk" again:

> YOU: (Same as before.) When I agreed to take you to the romantic comedy instead of the action movie I wanted to see, I did it because I wanted to make you happy ....

> SHE: (Same as before.) Okay, but you didn't have to be such a jerk about it ....

> YOU: (Slipping back into ICM because of the "jerk" comment) You know, if you're going to keep calling me a jerk, maybe I should go ahead and *be* a jerk and stop taking you to the movies. Next time let's just go to a movie *we both* want to see.

> SHE: You mean, you're not going to take me to any more romantic comedies?

> YOU: I just mean I don't see the point in taking you to a movie and then resenting it. I'm sorry this happened, and I don't want it to happen again. It's not good for either one of us, is it?

SHE: No, I guess not. (As you effectively shut her up, her dream of being a valuable enough woman to be romanced begins to wither. She then identifies in her mind a love-related activity that makes *you* feel valued as a man, and decides that she will henceforth stop providing it for you, or will provide it less often.)

Don't Allow Anger to Short-circuit Your Apology

In the above version of your apologetic conversation, you discussed your positive motivations and she responded by expressing her anger about the situation, as in the earlier example. But then you reacted badly to being called a jerk again, taking it personally instead of focusing on what that insult revealed about her depth of emotion. To resolve your own anger, your eventual response was to apologize for creating a situation where you ended up feeling resentful, and then you came up with a solution to ensure that you wouldn't feel that way again.

Your solution may sound reasonable enough on the surface, but it inspired her to plot revenge. Basically, your strategy was designed to take care of *your* anger and didn't even address *her* feelings. Still angry about her "jerk" comment, you failed to offer an important element of an effective apology: asking her to tell you all her related thoughts and feelings so that you could uncover her related key motivation – in this case, her deep desire for romance and her need to be honored and respected rather than scoffed at for wanting it – so that she could feel fully loved and valued as a woman. Without hearing her perspective at length, you formed a hasty solution that she's about to use against you.

Try Reinterpreting Your Focus

Sometimes when you're in a heated discussion with your woman and feelings are getting hurt, you can quickly bring yourself, and her, out of ICM by rethinking your attitude and reinterpreting your conversational focus.

As mentioned in Chapter 2, the focus of a conversation is subject to interpretation. When you first disagreed about the value of romantic comedies, you had a choice: to see your disagreement as a debate about the "truth" regarding romantic comedies, or to view it as just a difference of opinion. Misinterpreting an opinion-based disagreement as a Topic-focused debate is a common mistake. By misinterpreting your conversational focus as the "truth" of the Topic's value – in this case, the "truth" about the value of romantic comedies – you could go around and around disagreeing and never come to a resolution (see Example A).

Example A: Interpreting your conversation as Topic-focused:

Topic [Romantic Comedies (-)]   Topic [Romantic Comedies: (+)]

Self [You (+)]	Other [Her (-)]	Self [Her (+)]	Other [You (-)]
They're stupid! Basically, I'm right and she's wrong.	She thinks they're fun, and she expects me to think so, too. I guess that makes her a dingbat.	I love romantic comedies. They're totally fun, and they make me feel good.	He thinks they're stupid, but he's wrong. What a party-pooper. He's a jerk.

Whenever people talk, they're evaluated and judged by others. In particular, when people state their opinions as if they were facts, rather than having the humility and respect to allow for the reasonable possibility of other viewpoints, they can be judged quite negatively. On the above Focus Triangles, note that the values on corresponding angles all clash: whatever you view as good, she views as bad, and vice versa. By stating your clashing opinions of the topic as facts, you've created unnecessary friction. Although an argument about a movie may seem inconsequential, the value clashes all around indicate a serious degree of underlying relationship conflict.

To prevent this type of conflict, instead of engaging in a Topic-focused discussion about the "truth" of romantic comedies, you could recognize that the conversation is really a discussion about two different opinions, both of which are honest perspectives. By cultivating an opinion focus and recognizing that opinions are not universal truths, it's easier to acknowledge your differences respectfully and maintain positive Self and Other feelings. As mentioned previously, this becomes more difficult when the topic is close to either person's identity.

Example B shows how an opinion-focused discussion and the thinking behind it would look on your respective Focus Triangles. You can see how the focus of attention flows around and about each of the people and their respective opinions. In this case, you show respect for each other when you tell her that you don't like romantic comedies and she says she loves them. It's much easier to have a respectful conversation when you realize you're comparing opinions, not debating truths.

Example B: Interpreting your conversation as Opinion-focused:

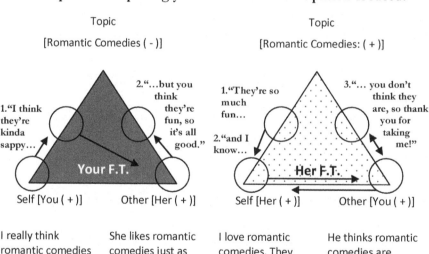

| Topic | | Topic | |
| [Romantic Comedies (-)] | | [Romantic Comedies: (+)] | |

1."I think they're kinda sappy... / 2."...but you think they're fun, so it's all good." / **Your F.T.** / Self [You (+)] / Other [Her (+)]

1."They're so much fun... / 2."and I know... / 3."... you don't think they are, so thank you for taking me!" / **Her F.T.** / Self [Her (+)] / Other [You (+)]

I really think romantic comedies are stupid. I've got a right to my opinion, but that's just my opinion, not an objective "truth."	She likes romantic comedies just as most women do, so I guess that makes her a normal woman, and I like women. She's got a right to her opinion.	I love romantic comedies. They make me feel good. But of course, that's just my experience, not everybody's.	He thinks romantic comedies are stupid, but that's normal for guys. He's good because he respects our differences and my right to my own taste. He wants me to have fun.

109

Consult Outside Resources

If you find yourself frequently unable to overcome ICM in your relationship, you may need to look for guidance from an outside resource before you'll be able to come up with winning solutions in your relationship. For example:

- ◆ Talk with a male friend, relative, or mentor who has a strong positive relationship with a woman and listen to the wisdom he has to offer.
- ◆ Sign up for a course on anger management.
- ◆ Seek the advice of a counselor, therapist, or other relationship expert.
- ◆ Read a self-help book.

In his self-help book *What You Feel, You Can Heal*, author and relationship expert John Gray describes three techniques for handling your difficult feelings and returning to positive ones. His techniques, which can help you increase your empathy toward your partner and *process* your anger rather than just controlling it, are called:

- ◆ The Duplication Technique
- ◆ The Anger Process
- ◆ The Love Letter Technique[12]

Read *What You Feel, You Can Heal* to learn about these techniques and find out how to use them to help yourself and heal your relationship.

Another self-help book you may benefit from reading is *The Peter Pan Syndrome* by Dr. Dan Kiley.[13] As simple-minded and possibly insulting as the title may sound, this book contains a brilliant literary analysis that offers relevant insights on the plight of men who experience continual failure in their hetero relationships, mostly because of the way they were raised. Kiley offers strong guidance for men who want to pull themselves out of this syndrome to increase their success with women, as well as guidance for the women and others in their lives who can play roles that support their efforts.

TALK ABOUT YOUR FEELINGS IN THE RIGHT WAY

It's only human to feel bad sometimes. Western women today encourage men to talk about their feelings, hoping to free them up from repression and enable them to live fuller lives. But when men try to talk to women about their negative feelings, it doesn't always work to their advantage.

You may or may not be accustomed to talking about your bad feelings, but if you are, and if you share your bad feelings with a woman *while you're still in the middle of feeling them*, she will probably see you as weak and try to help you feel better by shifting into a nurturing role. On the other hand, she could also respond to your apparent weakness by trying to take charge of you, thinking that you must need a leader – thus creating a power struggle. Either way, it would cast her into the role of your mother. Of course, feeling weak is a part of life. Your woman may feel comfortable nurturing or leading you on some occasions, such as when you get sick or when you're overstressed. However, if you feel weak frequently and talk about it regularly, your power dynamics within the relationship will be affected.

On the other hand, sharing aloud your feelings of positive desire and determination to act constructively will always make you sound strong. For instance, instead of dwelling on your vague, fearful/angry feeling that the world is against you, switch to talking about how you *want* to develop a winning attitude and how you feel *determined* to get yourself into a more positive frame of mind so that you can send out better vibes and attract more positive contacts in the world. If your woman is convinced that you will follow through, your attitude will allow her to relax and trust you – as long as you act according to your new plan.

In an apology, the same idea applies. If you begin an apology feeling okay about yourself but then slip into ICM during the conversation, remind yourself that you *want* to feel okay about yourself so that you can be effective in your relationship, and that you're *determined* to figure out how, even if you haven't done it yet. Before getting to the apology, you might need to extend the conversation by asking questions to gather more information, or you might need to just get away to think things over. If you need to step away from the situation, your woman will probably benefit from using John Gray's "Anger Process" or "Love Letter Technique" (referenced on the previous page) in order to process her immediate anger in a constructive way while you get some distance to sort things out.

Another successful approach to talking about your negative feelings is to time your conversation so that you're feeling calm and not overwhelmed by the emotion when you bring it up. For example, if you said to your woman, "I'm nervous about my job interview tomorrow," she might say something to try to help you feel better, but she'll probably also feel sympathetically nervous until your job interview is over. But if you waited until the job interview was over and then told her, "I was nervous going into the job interview this morning, but now that it's over, I feel okay," she would be able to appreciate your emotional honesty without feeling the need to mother you or suffer nervousness along with you. When you talk about your negative emotions after you've resolved them, you allow your woman to appreciate you for being human and admire you for dealing with your bad feelings in a strong way.

Finally, for those occasions when it's important to talk about a negative emotion right when it's happening, do your best to state what you're feeling without dramatizing it or acting it out. Then, if you can, offer some kind of reassurance. For instance, "I feel nervous about the job interview tomorrow, but I'm not going to let myself worry about it too much. I'm determined to do my best, and either way, everything will work out."

Identify Emotions

It may not always be easy to recognize exactly what you're feeling, especially if your parents never talked much about feelings when you were growing up. Furthermore, if you were raised to believe that showing your emotions is unmanly, you probably wouldn't have spent much time identifying them.

According to author and educator Daniel Goleman, though, developing emotional intelligence helps people succeed in many areas of life and is crucial for people who want to manage close personal relationships effectively.[14] In his bestselling book, *Emotional Intelligence: Why it can matter more than IQ*, Goleman says: "Self-awareness – recognizing a feeling as it happens – is the keystone of emotional intelligence."[15] When you're not aware of your own emotions, it may be difficult to identify them in others. And it makes sense that if you don't recognize your own feelings or the feelings of others, it would be pretty hard to manage your feelings, anyone else's feelings, or your relationship to that person.[16]

To build emotional self-awareness and more effectively handle feelings, Goleman suggests developing emotional awareness skills, including the following:

- Recognizing and naming your feelings
- Identifying the causes of feelings
- Recognizing the difference between feelings and actions[17]

Many resources are available for developing emotional intelligence. A quick search on the Internet will provide you with multiple options for emotional intelligence-related books, organizations, and training materials.

In practical terms, it may be best to begin with simple techniques for identifying your emotions. For instance, check yourself in the mirror whenever you feel an emotion that you can't necessarily name. If it's still not clear to you, ask someone to watch you and give you feedback on what she thinks you might be feeling, based on the way you look and sound. This could be your woman, a trusted associate, or a therapist. Or, just close your eyes, take a deep breath, ask yourself what you're feeling, and see if any words or images come to mind.

Another technique is to read through a long list of emotions and emotionally-charged attitudes, such as the list of emotions shown at www.emotionalcompetency.com/recognizing.htm, and see if any feelings listed there seem to fit your experience. There are other lists of emotions available on the Internet and elsewhere, so keep searching until you find one that speaks to you. In the same way that a multiple-choice test is easier to answer correctly than a fill-in-the-blank test, reading a list of emotions can make it a little easier to identify what you're feeling.

One simple exercise is to spend time watching a television drama with your woman and occasionally compare your opinions about what emotions the characters are expressing or hiding at any given moment. That would give you a chance to develop your perceptions together.

Process Your Bad Feelings Like a Strong Positive Leader

Some negative emotions make people feel weak: fear, humiliation, shame, confusion, inadequacy, and loneliness, to name a few. Other negative emotions, like anger, rage, vengeance, jealousy, hatred, and contempt, make people feel strong because they're fueled by a self-righteous attitude. Self-righteous feelings trigger an adrenaline rush that temporarily strengthens the body and creates a feeling of power. That power feels very good, nearly lifting the self-righteous person out of ICM – except that the person continues to feel bad because of whatever bad situation created the self-righteous reaction in the first place.

Depression is different. Depression has many clinical descriptions and manifestations, but I believe depression is the act of pushing down or suppressing bad feelings in an effort to stop suffering from them. Whatever negative emotions a depressed person is pushing down and trying not to feel lie hidden inside the person's mind/body and can potentially resurface. When they do, such feelings surface in layers of strength and weakness, causing the person to cycle back and forth between sounding and acting self-righteous and offensive, then weak and pitiful. Buried alive far below the surface of sad, depressed calmness and the underlying layers of negative emotion are very old dreams that were once bitterly abandoned and still cry out to be rediscovered and reclaimed. Reclaiming and actively pursuing those dreams is, in my opinion, the ultimate cure.

Unlike some emotional states, anger is one emotion that men can often identify when they're feeling it. If you feel angry and then quickly control your anger and process it mentally, you'll look strong to your woman. But if you use anger as an intimidation tool to get your way, or if you anger easily and find it difficult to control yourself, you might be surprised to know that, to her, you appear weak – personally deficient, either in moral character or in basic self-control. Because of this perception, she would probably try to control you as a mother would attempt to handle an unruly child. Or, if she felt too threatened by your anger, she might give in to your demands in order to protect herself, but would secretly look down on you and view herself as morally superior.

A strong positive leader deals with his anger and other emotions by owning them and then developing winning solutions. Developing winning solutions means thinking things out rationally, taking responsibility for your actions, and mastering the situation with fairness and wisdom so that you walk away looking decent, the kind of man a woman can believe in and would want to follow. All of this takes maturity.

If the idea of needing to mature as an adult sounds degrading or threatening to your dignity and freedom, consider your options. Strong positive leaders recognize that there are only two choices: either be willing to continue growing throughout life, or refuse to grow and allow your immaturities to limit your success.

Facing up to maturity issues, even as an adult, is probably the most powerful long-term strategy available for gaining power in a love relationship. Maturing means building character, and those who possess great character exude personal power and charisma.

As Stephen Covey wrote after researching all the literature on success published in the United States since 1776:

> ...almost all the literature in the first 150 years or so focused on what could be called the *Character Ethic* as the foundation of success – things like integrity, humility, fidelity, temperance, courage, justice, patience, industry, simplicity, modesty, and the Golden Rule . . . The Character Ethic taught that there are basic principles of effective living, and that people can only experience true success and enduring happiness as they learn and integrate these principles into their basic character.[18]

AVOID EMOTIONAL TRAPS

Sometimes when you owe an apology, or when your woman thinks you owe an apology, your conversation may go far beyond the bounds of the original problem. For example, imagine that after you make some simple goof or gaffe, she levels a wild accusation, calls you names, and then goes off topic, telling you a Poor Me story that sounds completely loony to you, where you're the villain and she's the victim. This kind of emotional outburst can trigger your anger, but it's possible to control your anger and remain calm by recognizing the trap and avoiding it – without having to let her know it.

115

Practically speaking, if her story sounds like fiction, maybe it is fiction. Recognizing this gives you a choice: to take her story literally and react by defending yourself and arguing with her over what's really true, or to appreciate her story as a creative, dramatic fictional tale that expresses a *kernel* of truth – perhaps a message about some of her deepest dreaded fears that she ultimately wants to be rescued from. In other words, she may be using storytelling to dramatize her hurt and scared feelings because she doesn't know how to express her emotions effectively in plain language.

In the next chapter, you'll learn more about fictional listening. This skill not only helps you step outside your own emotional space to keep your cool, but also enables you to bring the conversation in for a soft landing.

Do What It Takes

At times when nothing else seems to work, enlist others to help you resolve issues and get your emotions under control.

Switch Roles When Necessary

Ideally, when you talk about your feelings with your woman, you'll be able to turn your negative feelings into positive desires and determinations for future actions. In reality, though, you may have times when you can't do this no matter how hard you try because the bad feelings are too intense or too complicated.

Your need for an emotional healing may stem from indignities you've suffered directly from her. Maybe she insulted you or used you unfairly for her own selfish purposes in a way that's hard to get past. In that case, it only seems fair that she should listen to you talk about your viewpoint, apologize to you, and do whatever it takes to help you feel better.

On the other hand, if your need for an emotional healing stems from old traumas you endured as a child or as an adult in combat or another violent situation, your woman's help and understanding are critical but may not be enough. Traumas leave troublesome emotions and fragmented memory traces unprocessed and continually bouncing around in your mind/body. Emotional wounds caused by traumas, though not your fault, are yours to handle. You can either use them as an excuse for hurting others, or you can use them as an opportunity to learn how to heal yourself.

To resolve these kinds of feelings, team up with others, such as a therapist, an online resource, or a support group. You need others because, regardless of your IQ, it's usually impossible to singlehandedly untangle the web of dreaded memories and overwhelming feelings caused by a traumatic experience and then process them effectively. Working with others will help you reclaim your life sooner, and sharing your traumatic memories with others will help you feel less isolated. Gradually, you'll be able to share yourself more fully with your woman.

Generally, the only type of person who could or would be willing to team up with you to help you process those bad old issues would be someone who is heavily invested in your welfare. This might be a person who loves you and is deeply committed to you, a person who's been through something similar and can aid his own healing process by helping you heal, or a talented, capable professional who is invested in his mission of helping people with unresolved issues.

When you and your woman are having an emotional discussion and she says something that hits a sore spot and riles you up, it may be absolutely impossible to pull yourself out of your inner crisis by thinking through it at the time, or even by going off for a while to collect your thoughts. In fact, if your tendency is to space out and avoid dealing with emotional issues, or to brood and stew in your resentments and plot revenge, going off by yourself to try to talk yourself down from ICM might actually be counterproductive. On your own, you might generate even more anger or numb yourself out rather than cooling down and thinking clearly.

You might sometimes benefit from switching roles and allowing your woman to rescue you from ICM – *if* she can first feel centered and confident, and then view you in a positive, sympathetic light. This role reversal puts you in a position of weakness relative to her in an obvious way, but it also gives you a clear opportunity to showcase your courage and bravery in facing your challenges. As long as you're not apologizing at the time, having the courage to face up to your weak emotions will actually make you look morally strong from her perspective. If there's something you need to apologize for, though, it's still a good idea to wait until you feel more confident first.

Your combined effectiveness as a couple in pulling you out of ICM depends largely on how serious and complicated your emotional wounds and related behaviors are, how much you trust and care for each other, and what inner resources your woman brings to the relationship. Overall, if you have the courage to admit to your bad feelings when you can't sort through them on your own, you'll probably look stronger from her viewpoint by being honest than you would by trying to hide it. Hiding it could, in her eyes, make you look morally weak – and that's something she might easily use against you in the future.

Take Further Steps as Needed

Many extreme feelings are challenging to resolve. This class of feelings includes deep shame, humiliation, degradation, utter powerlessness, rage, terror, hopelessness, severe depression, extreme or frequent anger, anger toward the world, intense hatred, contempt, extraordinary fears, and deeply entrenched resentments.

These extreme negative feelings often lead people to do and say things that cause serious harm. They can drive your behavior off course even when you're not conscious of feeling them, and can gradually ruin your relationships with women and even your life. Because of this, talk to your woman about any extreme negative feelings you sometimes have so that she is at least aware of them and can recognize them when they surface in your behavior.

If you feel strong and powerful due to the self-righteous aspect of your extreme feelings, you might not want to seek help for fear of losing your power advantage when you're confronted with having to give up your self-righteousness. Remember, though: extreme self-righteous feelings can drive you to destroy your own life as well as the lives of others. There are ways to escape the cycle of self-righteousness and destructiveness, and constructive ways for you to feel powerful and good again without self-righteousness. Getting yourself there requires outside resources.

On the other hand, if your extreme feelings mostly make you feel weak, remember that your woman will probably see you as strong in a psychological or spiritual sense for having the courage to admit to them honestly. It's a good idea to collaborate with her when deciding how to deal with your situation. She will welcome your request for her ideas and insights. However, it wouldn't be fair to ask her to work singlehandedly to heal you, since by trying to be your healer as well as your woman, she could end up feeling overburdened and then take her frustrations out on you.

That's why it's important to do more than talk about your extreme feelings with your woman. She may be able to help you figure out root causes and heal in some areas, but when such feelings start to sabotage your relationship or your personal happiness, actively seek outside resources – books, Internet resources, a support group with a healing program such as AA, a psychologist, therapist, spiritual guide – someone or some group with the expertise to help you help yourself. Then make it clear to your woman that she doesn't need to worry about orchestrating your healing process because you're taking charge of your own recovery.

Even when you find yourself needing outside resources in addition to your woman's help to deal with old wounds, you can still project the image of being a team leader rather than a passive patient or a victim. Strong leaders in business and government seek advice from trusted experts and confidants all the time, so why shouldn't you? Since the old wounds caused by trauma were never your fault to begin with, there's no reason to avoid the problems they cause in your life now, just because you don't have an immediate solution. Form your team of consultants, communicate your vision of freeing yourself from the aftermath of old wounds, seek their advice and assistance, and empower them to help you achieve your vision. Ultimately, the key is to take control of the situation by accepting responsibility for doing whatever growth work is required to achieve a self-healing.

In this chapter you've learned techniques for handling your feelings during apology-related conversations. These include seeking winning solutions, developing emotional intelligence, and sometimes partnering with others to master your emotional challenges.

After you get your own feelings under control, you'll be in a position to learn how to handle your woman when *her* bad feelings cause problems during an apology-related conversation. There are ways to do it so as not to offend her, as you'll discover in Chapter 6.

6

HANDLING HER FEELINGS

Once your feelings are under control, you're ready to handle your woman's feelings in a way that both protects you and rescues her from being out of control.

If you think your choices are limited to either shutting her up or passively listening to her rant, you'll be glad to learn there's another way.

USE A SMART LEADERSHIP APPROACH

There may be times when your woman demands an answer or apology from you and then doesn't accept your response. This can happen when her negative feelings in Inner Crisis Mode are extreme. She might brush off anything you say because she wants to make *you* suffer the way you made *her* suffer so that you'll see how it feels – even though that strategy rarely, if ever, works. She might accuse you of terrible things that you didn't do, or call you offensive names that you feel are out of line. Then again, there might be some truth to her overblown accusations, making it harder for you to separate fact from fiction and stay calm. At these times, you have two separate sets of feelings to manage: hers and yours.

It's as if you're a lifeguard and she's a drowning swimmer. She wants you to rescue her from her horrible feelings, but when you try, she desperately pulls you under to try to save herself. If this seems like an unfair burden for you, remember: it's not a drowning swimmer's job to stop feeling desperate; it's the lifeguard's job to be stronger than the drowning swimmer and stay in control. If you let her dominate verbally and pull you under into ICM, then you'll both end up thrashing about and drowning together in your separate but equally bad feelings. However, if you're a strong swimmer in terms of your conversational strategy and can dominate her in the right way – not by pushing her underwater into ICM once again so as to save yourself, but by rescuing her from her "ocean of emotion" and carrying her back to safe ground without letting her drag you under – then you'll be her hero.

Keeping yourself above water might seem to be the hardest part of the whole rescue mission. Still, it's not enough. Even if you succeed in feeling okay about yourself no matter what she says about you, you still need to know how to help her process *her* emotions. Otherwise, if she eventually handles her own emotions without your help, she may not feel that she needs you quite so much – and then you're stuck with a less passionate relationship. A lifeguard who saves himself but fails to rescue the drowning swimmer can be commended for his good effort, but he still fails at his mission.

So your first challenge, once you feel okay about yourself and grounded in reality, is to get enough control of the conversation to maintain a leadership role while offering your woman opportunities to say all that she needs and wants to say. In this chapter, you'll learn how.

Dial Up Your Listening Skills

Whenever your woman seems to chatter endlessly about all her thoughts and feelings, you might wonder why you have to listen to it all. Often, she wants you to understand her experience and see what it's like to be her. Why does she want that? When you listen and understand how she thinks and feels, you give her a chance to process her experiences, help her feel less lonely, and provide her with attention that, to her, feels like love.

As your woman talks, your goal should be to understand how it feels to be her. Use your imagination to try to "walk a mile in her shoes." Instead of shutting her up or competing with her by talking about your own interests, try taking a moment to grasp what she's going through emotionally, even if it's not something you've ever gone through. Her experiences might sound inconsequential to you, but if you listen carefully, you might learn that some of them feel very important to her.

To get a feeling for how good or bad an experience feels to her, you might say, "Pretty good (or bad), huh?" or "On a scale of 1 to 10, how good (or bad) does that feel to you?" or "So, do you feel good or bad about that?" Then say something simple in a friendly way to show you're understanding the good or bad way it affects her, such as, "Well, good then" or "Yikes!" Then pause, watch, and listen sympathetically to see whether she feels that you understand her experience. If you give her quality attention in the moment, she's more likely to feel understood and feel better.

When she talks about something that's bothering her, be careful. If she doesn't feel you really understand or care about her feelings, then you might "flip a switch" in her mind. Instead of focusing on whatever problem she

123

was just describing, she might suddenly feel bad because she's convinced that you don't understand or care about her feelings. Now, she may feel you owe her an apology for not "caring" or not "listening." Or, she may go silent and secretly add your unsatisfactory reaction to her list of grievances that she will use against you at a later date.

When your woman talks to you about her concerns, handle her feelings by dialing up your listening and questioning skills as if you were her counselor. Give her your full attention and plenty of eye contact. Work to understand and respect her thoughts and feelings and don't interrupt too much. Check your understanding by rephrasing things she's said and ask if you've gotten it right. Ask her basic questions when you don't fully understand what she means. If she insults you for asking, it's not a sign that your question was bad, but rather a sign of how deeply bad she feels at that moment. Instead of getting mad about the insult, realize it's not about you and view it as a sign of how stuck she is in ICM.

It's in your own self-interest to check for understanding. That's because, if she thinks you don't understand her or decides you're not really listening or don't really care, she might get louder and more exaggerated in trying to get her points across to you and communicate how she feels about them. When this happens, reassure her that you want to understand and ask her questions until you do. Also, it's important to listen sympathetically. If you appear too analytical as a listener and don't respond in an outwardly caring and sympathetic manner, she'll end up feeling unloved and will probably use it against you at some point in the future – or right then.

Do Not Follow Her Negative Focus

The biggest mistake a man could make when his woman becomes angry and demands an apology is to allow her to lead the conversational focus. To handle her emotionality effectively, you'll need to listen to everything she has to say. However, when she sounds dramatic and off-base, you don't need to react or respond *literally* to what she says.

In the example below, which continues the movie argument theme, you make the mistakes of: 1) going along with the negative focus she places on you, and 2) taking her words literally.

SHE: You jerk! You let me choose what movie to see because you *claim* you wanted to make me happy, but then you made me feel stupid for enjoying it! Maybe subconsciously you don't *really* want to make me happy. You just want *your way all the time*, and you'll find *any way necessary* to make me suffer whenever you don't get your way so that, in the future, I'll just give in and go along. *You selfish pig!*

YOU: Now wait a minute. I am *not selfish!* That's totally unfair. Where do you get off analyzing my motives with your dopey psychobabble?

Instead of taking control of the conversational focus, you followed her lead and responded to her negative focus on you. Taking her words literally, you addressed her accusation directly and denied it. You asserted the principle of fair play and attacked her flawed analysis. Those moves may sound reasonable since she attacked you first and since her accusations were off-base. However, proving yourself right and proving her wrong in a personal conflict is just the Logical See-Saw Strategy, which doesn't end very well for anyone.

Yet, if you're not going to take her words literally, then how else would you take them?

Use Fictional Listening

To understand what fictional listening is, let's take a giant step backwards for a moment and look at the big picture of why each of you wanted a love relationship in the first place. Dreams of being married or being in a long-term love relationship often develop fairly early in life. Yours may have started when you decided to be like your dad, if your dad and mom were together. Or, maybe it started when you wished your dad and mom would live together happily. But in addition to your role models, another major influence in your life was probably stories that were told or read to you, as well as stories you read or watched on television or at the movies. Childhood stories, from fairy tales to cartoons, help to shape children's hopes and dreams. So to understand your basic relationship dreams and see how they compare with your woman's relationship dreams, it's a good idea to reflect on the nature of fictional stories.

In fiction, the purpose of a story is to communicate a kernel of truth in a way that will entertain and perhaps inspire viewers or teach a moral lesson. Fiction is designed for dramatic effect to tug at the emotions of readers and listeners, giving them a way to feel healed through catharsis or possibly challenging their ways of thinking. Fictional stories aren't designed to be taken literally since, by definition, they're not true. However, the deep truths they contain may be very meaningful.

For example, if you consider the American television series *The Adventures of Superman* from the 1950s, it isn't factually true that Superman ever existed or ever could exist. The story is entirely impossible. No man wearing a cape can fly at will. No man is more powerful than a locomotive or able to leap tall buildings in a single bound. But the story's deeper truth to young boys was that they had the potential to build themselves up to become extremely strong and powerful and could one day use their great strength to defend Truth, Justice, and the American Way – or other great values and virtues. In that sense, many boys "believed" in Superman.

Listening to that kind of fictional story helps boys dream an important dream that stimulates their good intentions and, even many years later, motivates a drive for excellence and heroism. The power of such a fiction is obviously great and good. So any boy who loved the Superman story when he was young would not have appreciated some stick-in-the-mud claiming that, in reality, the show was a lie. Of course, boys in the 1950s accepted the fact that Superman wasn't real. But to tell them that the story was a *lie* would have been unduly harsh. Such a literal interpretation of that fictional story might have undermined little boys' hopes for achieving the dream of one day being big and strong and doing great things as a grownup.

Boys' Stories vs. Girls' Stories

Boys usually favor stories in which the main character represents a superior man – either stronger and braver and faster than anyone else (like Hercules), able to outthink and outsmart everyone else (like Sherlock Holmes), or some combination of the two (like James Bond). In these stories, the hero usually saves someone's life, captures or kills the bad guys, and generally defeats the forces of evil. Girls or women, like the boys or men in this kind of story, are stereotypes of good or evil: good females might be innocent, vulnerable, and beautiful but in need of a rescue, or they might be helpful, friendly, intelligent sisterly types. Bad ones are usually powerful, cunning, aggressive, dangerous, and untrustworthy. Some bad ones are beautiful, some are ugly. The bad guys or forces of evil that appear in boys' stories include villains of either gender, monsters, space aliens, enemy combatants, or forces of nature, such as a wild animal or an avalanche.

By contrast, many of the stories favored by girls involve a beautiful princess or an innocent, lovely young girl who is threatened by an evil character, such as a wicked witch, a mean stepmother, a fire-breathing dragon, or a big bad wolf, and then rescued by a handsome prince or a brave woodsman or some similar character (like Snow White, Cinderella, Sleeping Beauty, or Little Red Riding Hood). The brave woodsman type of character is strong, kind, and able to defeat the enemy. The prince may be strong, brave, handsome, kind, and smart, but also usually has a large property inheritance and enjoys great wealth as well as power over people. Other girls' stories involve a beautiful, curious, and intelligent girl who, bored with home life, travels to a strange land and faces a variety of peculiar characters and perilous situations. She keeps her wits about her and meets various characters throughout her adventure who help her negotiate her way through the strange land and who aid her in returning home (like Alice in Wonderland or Dorothy from the Wizard of Oz).

It's pretty obvious that boys are often inspired by their favorite story characters to become great men who do great things. However, historically, it's not clear whether little girls, after hearing the traditional fairy tales, decide that they want to be beautiful, get into peril, and then look for a man to aid or rescue them, or whether fairy tales of this type were developed after countless generations of girls and women had lived out these types of dramas. Maybe both are true. Nevertheless your woman, as a girl, may have been inspired by similar stories to dream of growing up to be a beautiful woman who attracts a handsome prince or a good man to protect her from potential forces of darkness: an evil villain, an ugly monster, a big bad wolf, a wicked witch, a strange land filled with strange characters, or a life of poverty, abuse, and neglect.

So to use fictional listening with your woman whenever she goes on a tirade, imagine that you're witnessing a scene from a girls' fairy tale in the process of being reenacted. Listen to her as if she has cast herself in the role of a damsel in distress and is, in her own unique, creative way, acting out her drama with the hope of being rescued by a brave hero.

Fairytale Princesses, Superheroes, and Transformers

If you consider this possibility for a moment, you might wonder why your woman looks and sounds more like an ugly monster or a wicked witch during one of her dramatic outbursts than a beautiful, innocent damsel in distress. You might also wonder why, if she wanted to be rescued, she would cast you as an evil villain or a fire-breathing dragon that she herself tries to slay, rather than casting you as a handsome prince or brave woodsman who could do the fighting for her.

Part of the answer is that, in a fairy tale, there are multiple characters, whereas in your relationship there are only two actors – your woman and you. To act out her story, she may need you to play more than one role, and she too may need to act out multiple roles. In effect, you both reenact the story by becoming transformers. Another part of the answer is that you may be viewing her through the lens of your own boyhood adventure stories, where she suddenly looks to you like an evil enemy that must be overcome.

But why, you might wonder, would a woman want to act out a fairy tale by getting upset and going on a tirade? Doesn't that sound like a self-defeating approach?

Back in 1974, clinical psychologist and author Claude M. Steiner published a book called *Scripts People Live: Transactional Analysis of Life Scripts*. In it, Steiner explained that people often use characters from familiar stories as their models when developing a blueprint for their lives. He asserted that storybook scripts are adopted by young children and that a person's inner child, which remains intact throughout life, remembers this storied way of thinking and plays out the chosen script.[19]

If, as Steiner suggested, both boys and girls adopt scripts from storied characters to use as lifetime blueprints, then this explains why men who modeled themselves after a superhero would try to do good deeds, win competitions, and generally act heroically. Likewise, any woman who long ago dreamed of being a beautiful princess living in the castle of her husband, the handsome prince, may think of herself as a princess when she pampers herself, decorates her beautiful home, and goes shopping for a beautiful gown to wear when going out to a social event with her husband. Playing a superhero, a princess, or any other positive storybook character represents a childhood dream, a dream that shapes people's identities and provides key motivations for behavior in adulthood.

Steiner didn't suggest in his book that a woman's tirade might be an attempt to act out a dramatic episode based on a fairy tale. In fact, he warned against the idea of rescuing others.[20] However, every girl's fairy tale has some evil character or some threat to the heroine. Therefore, it stands to reason that, from her inner child's perspective, a woman's tirade may express the horrifying moment when her favorite fairytale heroine faces the evil threat.

Happily Ever After – Not

Most people understand that a young woman's dream of being a beautiful fairytale princess and finding her Prince Charming is normally played out when she gets married. It's easy to see that having a beautiful wedding would be extremely fun for a woman. She gets to be the center of attention, wear a beautiful gown, receive a lot of gifts, and feel loved. On the level of her inner child, she gets to finally make a childhood dream of getting married and living happily ever after come true.

After marriage, a woman usually follows her story's script by attempting to live happily ever after. However, most real marriages and long-term relationships don't continue that way for long. In reality, women in marriages and other long-term relationships find themselves in all sorts of peril. Real-world dangers include being relegated to the drudge work of running a household, often feeling somewhat abused or neglected by her family (like Cinderella); dealing with cruel relatives and going through the motions of an unfulfilling life as if in a kind of trance or stupor, a sort of living death somehow imposed by a relative's constant cruelty (like Sleeping Beauty or Snow White); or being ogled, chased, and cornered at work by a predatory man with enough influence to get her fired for not allowing him to consume her (like Red Riding Hood). These situations stimulate a woman's inner child and childhood scripts, making her feel that she's stuck in the bad part of a storybook tale and needs to be rescued by a hero.

Similarly, a young woman who's bright and curious may feel she's reached the happy ending of her *Alice In Wonderland* fairytale script when, as an adult, she meets and marries or lives with a man who gives her a sense of home, respects her intelligence, and helps her understand and negotiate the strange world around them. However, if she later begins to feel critical of him and decides that he, too, is a strange character, she may suddenly feel that she's once again lost in Wonderland. She may then try to find "a way home" by making a new home with someone else – someone she considers more normal, respectful, and loving – someone who will give her a greater sense of safety, security, and belonging.

When your woman is on a tirade, it might be difficult to tell which story she's playing out or why. However, if you're being cast as an evil villain or monster or strange character, you'll probably sense *that* right away. Then you'll know that some kind of dramatic story has taken over her consciousness and that she's trying to act it out with you.

The question is: how should you respond?

Respond as the Story's Hero

Let's go back to our romantic movie argument and see how you could interpret your woman's words differently by using fictional listening. Once again, here's what she said to you:

> SHE: You jerk! You let me choose what movie to see because you *claim* you wanted to make me happy, but then you made me feel like a dope for enjoying it! Maybe subconsciously you don't *really* want to make me happy. You just want to *get your way all the time*, and you'll find *any way necessary* to make me suffer whenever you don't get your way so that, in the future, I'll just give in and go along. *You selfish pig!*

From what she said here, it's not clear what fairy tale or drama she might be acting out. What you do know is that she's coming up with a wild fiction and has cast you as the jerk and selfish pig, clearly a bad guy, and clearly not true. You also see, from the look on her face, that she's upset – a damsel in distress. You can tell that she's angry and you guess from what she's saying that she feels put down as well. That makes you feel somewhat sympathetic. On the other hand, though, she's blaming you, accusing you of something bad that isn't true, and that makes you feel unsympathetic and inclined to put a stop to it. Yet you know that if you put a stop to it, you'd be silencing her, and she wouldn't end up feeling good about that. Also, you realize that she may try to use your reaction against you in the future.

With fictional listening, you now have a choice. Instead of responding to her negative focus on you by taking her blame statements literally and defending yourself, or by going on the attack as if you were the "good guy" who is falsely accused of being the "bad guy" (from your own boyhood fictional stories), you can choose to help her play out her drama and get to the resolution. To do this, you would use your transformer capacity to take the heroic lead while temporarily allowing her to address you as the bad guy.

Responding as the story's hero means stepping into the dramatic action as the hero of her story and setting a new, positive tone. As her hero, you'd act generous and sympathetic toward her. Remember, you're acting, so instead of responding to her logically when she erroneously accuses you of being the bad guy, realize that she's confused and focus directly on her in a positive, sympathetic way. Ask her how bad she feels and let her cry on your shoulder and tell you her Poor Me story.

Tips from *Men Are From Mars, Women Are From Venus*[21]

"A woman…seeks relief by expressing herself and being understood."

"By learning to listen, gradually [you] will experience that she will appreciate [you] more even when at first she is upset with [you]."

"If she does not feel understood then it is difficult for her to release her hurt."

"…blaming does not work."

As a transformer, you need to allow her to treat you as the bad guy at first – because to act out her story, she needs you to play that role – until, once you've helped her enough, she suddenly recognizes, to her great relief, that you're really the hero after all.

Don't Miss the Healing Opportunity

Keep in mind that *she may not be aware* of acting out a fictional tale. But whether or not she realizes that she's off in another dimension, she needs you to take her *feelings* seriously and help her process them. You can't do that by making her painfully aware that, logically, you think what she's saying is just a fiction, or especially by mocking or criticizing her for being overly dramatic.

Remember how boys who love Superman feel about hearing some old stick-in-the-mud claim that the Superman myth is a big *lie?* Such a literal criticism could undercut a boy's dream of growing up to be big and strong and could destroy his childlike hope of one day becoming a great man.

Well, the same principle applies to the inner child inside a woman. If you were to suggest that her Poor Me story was just a bunch of hooey, a big lie, her inner child might easily interpret your statement to mean that her favorite fairy tale from childhood, the very blueprint of her life, was a lie. Deep inside, she may conclude that you're saying she will never achieve her childhood dream of being loved by a heroic man. Her inner child might hear your criticism as implying that she isn't really beautiful or deserving of a handsome prince. Similarly, she may believe that you feel she doesn't deserve your love, affection, and respect, or that you don't really care enough about her to rescue her from her distress – because these are all elements of the childhood story reverberating in the back of her mind. These ideas could undercut her motivation for being with you, making her reconsider the things she does to make some of *your* relationship dreams come true. Also, if you said that you thought she was being irrational or acting out a fictional drama, you would disrupt the storytelling healing process that she needs to be led through.

There's a better way for you to respond, provided you do so with a sympathetic attitude rather than a sarcastic tone:

YOU: (Switching the conversational focus from a negative focus on you to a sympathetic focus on her and her bad feelings, and staying "above water" as her hero/lifeguard by realizing she's in ICM) Wow, is that what you think? It sounds like you're really afraid that I don't care how you feel. It seems you're afraid that, just like some selfish pig, I would do absolutely anything to get my way, even at the expense of your feelings. It sounds like you're worried that you were wrong about me, and that all along I've been a jerk *pretending* to be a nice guy. Is that what you're afraid of?

In the above example, here are some of the things you've just done right:

- Seeing that she was in ICM, you remained confident and strong even in the face of her abusive accusations.
- You used fictional listening and recognized that you could play a positive role as her hero.
- When she focused negatively on you, you tolerated it but, like a transformer, you led the conversational focus away from yourself and toward her in a positive, understanding, sympathetic way.
- You identified that she was acting out a story of being the damsel in distress who temporarily saw you as a selfish bad guy who had fooled her into believing you were a good guy. You gave her a chance to discover – on her own – that you're really a good guy after all.
- When you listened to her accusations, you reinterpreted her statements in terms of her fears and insecurities so that you could begin to figure out her underlying motivations – not: "It sounds like you *think* I'm just a selfish pig! Is that what you're saying?!" but: "It sounds like you're *afraid* that I'm just a selfish pig. Is that your fear?"
- By acting like a transformer – playing the hero while temporarily letting her address you as the bad guy – you allowed her to both doubt you and rely on you to rescue her, a truly heroic feat.
- You resisted the temptation to initiate a Topic-focused argument about "what is true" or "what happened" in your relationship. Instead, you recognized that your role was to rescue her value and pull her out of ICM by focusing on her fictional story so that you could listen for clues revealing her fears. This would enable you to identify her associated hopes and dreams.

Consider Her Stories

To reiterate, women sometimes make bold accusations when, in fact, they are really voicing their deepest fears and insecurities – testing out a dark alternative theory of their man's motivations to see how he reacts to it. Your woman will be watching you carefully to see how you react to her fear-driven accusations, and will see your reaction as an important indication of whether those accusations might be true. Seeing you react in anger might convince her that her worst fears are more likely to be true.

Most people develop a narrative or storyline in their mind about the story of their life. Many of us have at least two stories going: a Victorious Me story and a Poor Me story based on different sets of facts (or imagined "facts") from our lives. Part of the time we may think we're pretty great and quite possibly the best person around. At other times we may suddenly worry that our lives are going wrong, we're headed for failure, life is unfair, and our *real* life story is a gripping tragedy.

Throughout life, people with multiple narratives identify with first one story and then the other in an effort to determine which one is true. Such is the case for women who switch back and forth between self-confidence and insecurity.

For your woman, the story of her life as she's trying to compose it in her mind may be based largely on her success in her love relationship(s). This is probably not true for all women, but at least for a large number of women, their fondest hopes and dreams are connected to loving and being loved. Your woman's dark theory about your ulterior motives could be quite frightening to her, as it would shatter her dreams if it proved to be true.

Your woman will always compare the story of her life at any given moment with the fairytales she loved as a child and adopted as her own. On a good day, she feels hopeful that the story of her life will end up close enough to those stories. On a bad day, when she fears the worst about her fate, she can become overwrought with emotion and wish that you would ride in on your white horse and rescue her.

The things women and men want from relationships are often so very basic, and sometimes so childlike, that we may have trouble admitting to them because we're embarrassed.

For instance, your woman may not want to tell you, "I want to feel special!" or "I want you to think I'm beautiful!" because she might be afraid that you would laugh at her for being so naïve and unsophisticated. Bear in mind, though, that your dreams of being a superhero or maybe a James Bond type could be considered equally naïve, and yet such dreams may motivate much of your behavior, both personally and professionally.

> **Key Motivations from *Men are from Mars, Women are from Venus*[22]**
>
> "Women are motivated and empowered *when they feel cherished.*"
>
> "Men are motivated and empowered *when they feel needed.*"
>
> "Women need to receive caring, understanding, respect, devotion, validation, reassurance."
>
> "Men need to receive trust, acceptance, appreciation, admiration, approval, encouragement."

Once again, here's what you've both just said, and here's how you ultimately help her back to good feelings:

> SHE: You jerk! You let me choose what movie to see because you *claim* you wanted to make me happy, but then you made me feel like a dope for enjoying it! Maybe subconsciously you don't *really* want to make me happy. You just want to *get your way all the time*, and you'll find *any way necessary* to make me suffer whenever you don't get your way so that, in the future, I'll just give in and go along. *You selfish pig!*

> YOU: (Not taking it personally, and marveling at the depth of her fears) Wow, is that what you think? It sounds like you're really afraid that I don't care how you feel – and that, just like some selfish pig, I would do absolutely anything to get my way, even at the expense of your feelings. It sounds like you're afraid that you were wrong about me, and that all along I've actually been a jerk *pretending* to be a nice guy. Is that what you're afraid of?

> SHE: (Calming down a little because you've read her emotions correctly) Well, it sure seemed like it. It really hurt when you made

135

me feel stupid for enjoying the movie. Your attitude took all the fun out of the evening for me. Thanks a lot! (She's still in ICM to some extent, but she's given you a clue about one of her key motivations in her relationship with you: fun.)

YOU: (With empathy) That must've felt terrible. And I know what you mean about having fun. I want us to keep having fun together, too. What was the most fun part of the movie for you?

SHE: (Hesitantly) Well, I loved the ending. I love happy endings.

YOU: (Being encouraging, respectful, and positive) Happy endings make you feel good, huh? Well, I like it when you feel good. What other parts of the movie were fun for you?

SHE: (Smiling) Well, I love the romance of it – the beautiful scenery and costumes, the beautiful people, the way things always work out in the end – the way love should be.

YOU: Well, I'm glad you enjoyed it. I have to admit that I never quite understood why women like romantic comedies so much. They've always seemed unrealistic to me, not the way love really is. But I guess you could say that action movies are pretty unrealistic, too.

SHE: That's right!!!

YOU: I'm sorry I spoiled your fun. I didn't mean to. It's frustrating that we have fun in different ways sometimes – but the important thing is that we can still share fun things together and not be selfish about it. I definitely don't want to be selfish, and if I sometimes come across that way, I'm sorry. I don't ever want to make you feel like your fun isn't important to me – but I also don't want to give up my kind of fun.

SHE: I agree. To be happy together, we both need to keep having fun, and sometimes that means taking turns. We're going to your movie next week, right?

Now that the conversation is over, here are more things you've done right:

- You learned that she dreams of a relationship with you in which you have fun together. You also learned that she feared you might not care whether she has fun anymore at all, as long as you're having fun. After learning this, you successfully reinforced your desire to see that she has fun, too. You asked her questions so that she could reminisce about fun parts of the movie and so that she could feel loved by sharing it with you and seeing your positive response to her good feelings.

- By tolerating her dramatic fiction about you as the selfish pig/jerk, you've done her the service of bringing to light some of her deepest, darkest fears instead of rejecting or blaming her for feeling them. This helped her feel that you truly care about her emotions and that you love and accept her even when she's hurt, frightened, and confused.

- Your willingness to play along in her dramatic conversation (not as a victim following her negative lead, but as a strong positive leader choosing a positive Other focus until she felt better) helped her feel safe to work through her dramatic feelings and say what she needed to say so that she could quickly come down from her worst fears and begin to talk to you more rationally again.

- You apologized for making a comment that made her feel bad, but you didn't apologize for being selfish or being a jerk. Instead, you stayed true to yourself to maintain your dignity. You expressed sympathy: "That must've felt terrible." And you later made a hypothetical apology statement: "...if I sometimes come across that way [selfishly], I'm sorry...." This "if-then" statement served to emphasize your positive desire to be a good guy and not a selfish one, which was a strong way for you to share your feelings of positive desire and determination. But you never actually said that you *were* selfish, because you weren't.

- You listened to her and asked her questions with the goals of: 1) giving her positive, appropriate attention to help her feel better, and 2) finding out what relationship dream of hers was shattered or threatened (in her view) by your criticism of the romantic comedy, so that you could help her affirm her relationship dream and feel reconnected to it. (She dreams that you are a good man, a "handsome prince" who loves her unselfishly, respects and occasionally indulges her need for romance, and cares about seeing that you both have fun rather than one having fun at the other's expense.)

The Healing Power of Fiction

Do stories or dramas that are reenacted really have healing power? Aristotle thought so. In a work of non-fiction called the *Poetics*, he wrote about the emotions of pity and fear. He said that a well-written tragic play causes viewers to feel both pity and fear as they identify with the tragic hero. Feeling these emotions as they watch the drama, he said, allows viewers to experience emotional catharsis, or a purging of the emotions.[23]

Purging, of course, is the idea of flushing out toxins – in this case, emotional toxins. As stated on wiseGeek.com: "Drama can evoke powerful emotions, and people who watch it and are moved leave the theater clean, refreshed, and purified in emotional experience."[24]

Interestingly, two of the most prominent emotions hidden under the surface of anger – when anger is not just a manipulative bullying tactic – are the same two emotions noted by Aristotle: pity and fear. Pity takes the form of the angry person's self-pity, and fear is a fear that the angry person's dreams are being crushed or simply might never come true.

When your woman called you a jerk and a selfish pig, beneath the anger she felt hurt by the way you made fun of the movie she enjoyed. She thought you were unkind and unfair, and she therefore felt sorry for herself – pitied herself. To her, your behavior showed that you thought her dream of finding romance, just as her favorite childhood fairytale heroine did, was absurd and laughable rather than precious and dear. Her underlying fear was that you might not be the nice guy – the Prince Charming – that she originally hoped and dreamed you were. She worried that she might have made a big mistake in judging your character, and that beneath your outer appearance you might really be uncaring and selfish. These fears threatened to bring her relationship dreams crashing down. She may even have feared that you thought she wasn't really as beautiful or lovable as the fairytale princess she always dreamed of being when she was a little girl.

Simply feeling the feelings of pity and fear won't automatically provide a cathartic healing. Clearly, many people get stuck in bad feelings and don't know how to get over them. Throughout society there are those who indulge in self-pity as a lifestyle choice. And plenty of folks walk around feeling frightened of all sorts of things without ever being able to resolve their fears. People who have known extreme misfortune might find themselves sometimes filled with random anger, self-pity, and fear in a seemingly endless loop of toxic emotions that they don't know how to resolve. Often these people need professional help far beyond a catharsis.

What brings on a catharsis or emotional healing through fictional listening is not just experiencing the pity and fear, but being filled with these emotions during a reenactment of the entire drama, from the setup of a distressing situation to the dramatic climax and resolution where the dream is restored. It's a little different than the catharsis of watching a Greek tragedy, where you empathize with the tragic hero but go home to your own life. In fictional listening, your woman is the main character in her drama, and working toward a tragic ending wouldn't be healing for her. Her story has to end happily or hopefully to be healing, more like a fairy tale.

Your woman's drama is her cry for help – her call for a hero to rescue and love her. To silence her and refuse to rescue her would be the equivalent of trapping Dorothy in the Wicked Witch's castle forever, always on the verge of being killed, or keeping Sleeping Beauty locked up in the thorny castle tower to sleep for the full 100 years, instead of allowing the drama to unfold until she's awakened with a kiss and her happiness is restored. These stories would be as bad to her as the idea would be to you of seeing Superman, Indiana Jones, Harry Potter, or any other favorite hero permanently defeated and utterly humiliated. Such bad endings represent to the inner child the victory of hatred over love, or evil over goodness.

In your relationship, if your woman has unprocessed feelings of anger, self-pity, and fear, her bad feelings would be trapped inside her body/mind and would cause trouble. From time to time they would rise to the surface, continually bringing down the quality of your relationship.

To help her use drama to process her anger-related emotions, lead her through these feelings if and when they arise. Listen sympathetically through your secret transformer capacity and refuse to take her dramatic exaggerations literally or personally. Keep the conversation positive Other focused until you understand her fears, hopes, and relationship dreams. Then support her dreams and renew her hopes of achieving them.

If her fictional tale contains elements of nonfiction, acknowledge that they're real issues but keep the focus on her drama. Later, after her dramatic outpouring is done and she's ready to speak to you in a logical way, you can discuss those concerns separately.

Should you find that your best attempts at fictional listening fail to help her resolve her anger or correct her erroneous perceptions of you, the problem may be due to an unresolved trauma from her past. In that case, encourage her to seek help from outside resources.

UNCOVER HIDDEN EMOTIONS AND PROVIDE INTERVENTIONS

In Chapter 2 you saw a chart detailing various inner experiences of anger and interventions for dealing with your woman when she's angry. In this section, you'll read further information about the interventions.

Help Her Rekindle Hopes and Dreams

The painful cascade of emotions often hidden beneath your woman's outer expression of anger involves pity and fear: self-pity for whatever hurt or loss she's experienced and fear that she can't become the beloved woman she always dreamed of being, or fear that some other important dream will never come true. You've also learned that, just underneath her fear, a tenuous layer of hope exists – hope that her dream could still come true. And you've learned that, if you correctly identify her dream, you can encourage, reinforce, and renew her hopes of making her dream come true. This should help her calm down and feel confident again.

Help Her Rethink Expectations

The anger chart in Chapter 2 also offers an intervention to use when your woman's anger is a long-term issue that comes up again and again, based on her demand to understand *why* some painful event in the past occurred. For instance, maybe when you got married years ago, you showed up to your wedding an hour late, and now every time she gets upset she brings it up and pleads with you to explain: "Why did you do that to me?"

You might think that if only you could apologize for your wedding-day tardiness in the right way, and if only she could forgive you this time, you could both let it go. But in many cases, a person's anger stems not from a failure to forgive but from harboring unrealistic expectations. To diffuse that kind of anger, help her look back at the situation and retroactively adjust her expectations to be more realistic. Discuss your wedding day with her and help her see that, although her expectation that you would arrive promptly back then seemed perfectly reasonable at the time, she now needs to rethink that expectation. After all, her expectation of you back then failed to take into account your actual state of mind and emotions that day. Gently help her realize that her expectation of you on your wedding day was actually not realistic, given who you were then. Once she adjusts that past expectation, ask her to talk about any other issues related to the wedding. Finally, gently switch the focus of conversation to discuss her current hopes, dreams, and expectations of you now. Reassure her that you're committed to meeting her expectations as long as she's committed to accepting your imperfect but honest efforts. By working hard to keep up your end of the bargain, you'll earn the right to ask her to trust and accept you.

Help Her Find a Broader Answer

In other cases, unmet expectations may not be connected to a disappointing event, but to a dream that is dying. For instance, maybe she always dreamed that one day you'd make her rich and buy her a palatial home in a wealthy area; however, now she's realizing that this dream may never come to pass. Lately, whenever she feels lousy, she gets angry and blames you all over again for failing to make that dream come true. To help her grow and resolve her anger, recognize that she's deep in ICM and find a way to maintain your dignity and good opinion of yourself through self-acceptance. Then diffuse the anger by helping her put things into perspective and see the bigger picture of her life.

To get a sense of the big picture of her life, ask her about all the dreams she holds dear. It may help to make a list of those dreams to examine whether they might conflict with each other. For example, maybe she wanted to become rich and live extravagantly, but she also dreamed of raising a large family. Early in your marriage, you acted on supporting her dream of having a large family by having nine children together. Unfortunately, having nine children got in your way of becoming rich and living extravagantly. Given the nature of those different dreams, and given your career path, you could call her attention to the difficulty of having both.

Another way to look at the big picture is to ask about her sense of purpose in life. Your goal is to discover how her life's purpose might clash with the dream of hers that she now fears may never come true. For instance, if she always dreamed of being rich but feels that her purpose in life is to serve humanity, it's possible that, given her personality, becoming wealthy would have provided too many tempting diversions that would have distracted her from achieving her life's purpose. On the other hand, her purpose of serving humanity would appear to fit well with her goal of having a large family, since family life has offered her many opportunities to serve others on the family and community levels. In other words, the dream that you made happen – having a large family – was in line with her self-identified life's purpose, whereas her dream that you didn't make happen – being rich – may not have aligned with her purpose, given her personality. The clash between these various big-picture considerations could reveal the "final cause" that explains why one of her dreams didn't materialize: it wouldn't have fit with her higher purpose in life.

People rarely find that every single dream of theirs comes true, and yet this doesn't mean they can't be happy. For those dreams of your woman's that died or are dying, you might be able to diffuse her anger by helping her see her life in the bigger picture.

This does *not* mean berating her for having too many dreams, telling her bluntly that she should be happy with what she's got, or handing her your diagnosis of her spiritual purpose without her input! Instead, begin by making sure you feel confident and good about yourself in spite of your limitations in your ability to provide for her and regardless of her anger. Then make sure you see her sympathetically, as a woman having an inner crisis who needs to be rescued, while positioning yourself as the transformer/hero or the lifeguard who wants to rescue her. Next, interview her to learn of her dreams and thoughts about her purpose(s) in life. Finally, express sympathy and understanding as you help her piece together the bigger picture of her life and gently suggest that some dreams might fit the bigger picture better than others do. This could help her come to terms with saying goodbye to some of her old dreams, making room to dream a new dream together or to refocus pleasantly on other dreams you share. That will leave you both feeling better.

Help Her Become a Better Person

You also saw in Chapter 2 that your woman's anger could be a clever game – a self-righteous tantrum that she uses to intimidate you whenever she can't get her way by other means. The main intervention is:

1. Catch her at her game in a firm but loving way.
2. Refuse to reward her for it.
3. Teach her the steps she needs to take to get what she wants.
4. Teach her the limits of what she can expect to get.

However, if she's a really good actress and knows how to pretend to feel hurt and fearful, you might wonder how you would know whether her feelings are real or just an act.

One way to know is to think about how well she generally handles herself whenever things don't go her way. If she's normally gracious about taking turns and acts mature when things don't go her way, her occasional anger is likely to cover up real feelings – a genuine response to a sense of injustice. On the other hand, if she often gets angry, pouty, or dramatic whenever she can't get what she wants, she's being manipulative. In that case, her character would benefit (in spite of her protests) if you called her out on her immature behavior. Without blaming her excessively (because her manipulative personality was formed during childhood through a combination of her nature, her upbringing, and the role-models she chose, not engineered by conscious choice), firmly teach her clear rules of adult behavior for getting the things she wants and enforce the rules vigorously. Also, reward her with positive attention whenever she handles disappointments graciously, as any good parent would do. If she's beyond your ability to influence with these efforts, she may not be right for you.

Look for Other Emotional Layers

Sometimes emotions cover up other emotions. For example, one fear can cover up another fear: your woman might be afraid of talking to you about her need for more of your attention because she fears that she might be rejected, which hides her fear of being divorced, unloved, and alone, as well as her fear of losing status and facing the working world or going into poverty and homelessness, which hides her fear of premature death. On the other hand, if your woman is a pool shark challenging you to a game of pool, the fear she exhibits of losing the next game to you might cover up feelings of extreme confidence, amusement, and contempt. To find out what emotions are hiding beneath your woman's expressed feelings, ask her to tell you more about them and listen carefully for clues. Of course, just hearing what she says isn't enough; her behavior has to match her words.

Negative emotions that make a person feel strong are often used to cover up negative emotions that make the person feel weak. Anger that covers up self-pity and fear is a perfect example. Excessive suspiciousness may hide feelings of guilt or fearfulness. Jealousy may hide a lack of self-acceptance and an inability to appreciate the person's own value outside a competitive framework in which she is deemed the best. According to Michael Lewis, author of *Shame: The Exposed Self*, expressions of rage or a state of depression may be caused by underlying feelings of deep shame.[25] And according to philosopher Eli Siegel, author of *Self and World: an Explanation of Aesthetic Realism*, the attitude of contempt is "a disposition in every person to think he will be for himself by making less of the outside world."[26] In other words, contempt involves a failure to acknowledge the full positive value of others, of the world, or of life itself. Since contempt is a self-righteous attitude based on views that are neither accurate nor fair, it may cover up intellectual weakness. Another way of looking at contempt is that it may cover up an overwhelming sense of feeling cheated by life, which leads the person to conclude that life isn't fair or good. This is an erroneous but understandable generalization of a bad personal experience to all of life.

The drive or urge to abuse power may at times cover up feelings of powerlessness or inadequacy. Excessive controlling behavior may cover up feelings of pronounced distrust of other people or of life itself, as well as the deep fears that accompany such entrenched distrust. Hostility may cover up feelings of isolation and loneliness. On the other hand, according to Martha Stout, author of *The Sociopath Next Door: the Ruthless Versus the Rest of Us*, any of these self-righteous negative feelings, behaviors, and attitudes in people with sociopathic tendencies may be tools of manipulation fueled by a lust for domination over others and the thrill of winning, with no depth of emotion hidden underneath.[27]

When your woman is upset, it's important to maintain control of the conversational *focus* while listening and asking questions to find out all the different things she feels and thinks and needs to talk about. As the conversational leader, you should apply the appropriate intervention when she expresses anger by identifying the type of anger. Finally, identify other emotional layers, if applicable, to increase your insight and potentially stimulate her greater self-awareness.

Next, Chapters 7 and 8 contain snapshots of apologies from men to women. There you'll see apology lines you've probably used in the past. Not only will you read about the pros and cons of each example, but you'll see how a woman might perceive it differently than a man does.

H<small>OW TO</small> A<small>POLOGIZE TO</small> Y<small>OUR</small> W<small>OMAN</small> . . .

7

TYPICAL APOLOGIES:
PART I

When you deliver an apology, you never know: Will she accept it? Pretend to accept it? Or reject it *in your face*? To improve your chances of success, this chapter examines various typical apologies in three out of four categories: the incomplete apology, the over-apology, and the non-apology. The fourth category, the complete apology, will be featured in Chapter 8.

In this chapter and the next, you'll see what's right and wrong with each typical apology and how each one looks from a woman's vs. a man's perspective.

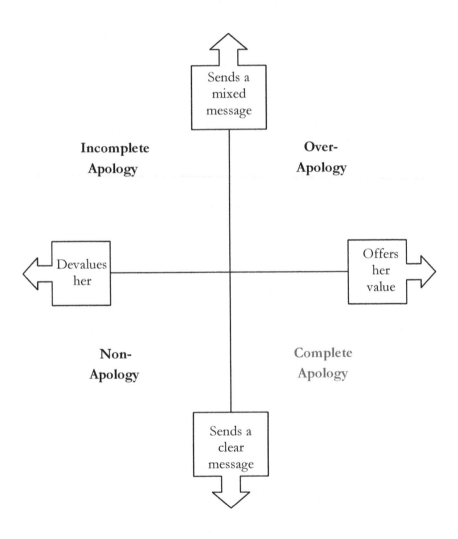

INCOMPLETE APOLOGIES

An incomplete apology offers some value but leaves out one or more critical elements. Women's reactions to them vary. Some women reject and criticize them, often very rudely. Other women accept them verbally while secretly resenting them, possibly planning to get even. Still others decide that incomplete apologies are better than none at all and accept them with sadness and resignation.

As you read through this section, you might notice that these apologies seem to work well enough for you in some situations – maybe with other men who use the same kinds of apologies. But in a close personal relationship with a woman, one of the biggest problems in delivering an incomplete apology is that, long term, it can have a negative effect on both of you.

Even if she accepts your incomplete apology at the time you deliver it, she probably won't feel healed by it, which means that her emotional wound could reopen at a later date. This would compel her to bring up the issue again. Or, if she never brings it up again, she may have given up on you to some extent, losing some of her passion for you in the process. For those women who reject your incomplete apology out of hand or accept it in a resentful and critical way, the apology itself, though not without merit, might be used against you anyway. And that's on top of her need to continue complaining about the underlying issue that your apology was intended to handle.

The incomplete apologies we'll look at here are the *Hypothetical* Apology, the *Vague* Apology, and the *Poor Me* Apology.

The Hypothetical *Apology*

The *Hypothetical* Apology is an "if-then" statement. The speaker may use it to express regret for possible bad feelings that may have been caused by his behavior, although he doesn't specifically admit to wrongdoing. If the expression of regret isn't stated, it could be implied through the speaker's sympathetic tone of voice, facial expressions, or other non-verbal means.

This type of apology can also be categorized as a non-apology, since it can be delivered coldly and may be used as a way of denying any wrongdoing. The way to categorize and interpret it in a specific case depends on the tone used and on what's implied nonverbally.

Examples:

- "If I hurt you in any way, I'm sorry." (*If* I hurt you, *then* I'm sorry.)
- "I apologize for anything I said that may have offended you." (*If* I offended you by anything I said, *then* I apologize.)
- "Please excuse any misbehavior on my part." (*If* I misbehaved, *then* please excuse me for it.)

What's right about it?	• The speaker admits the possibility of wrong-doing.
	• He shows that he's aware of possibly offending or hurting the woman and that he's willing to express his concern or regret out loud.
	• He shows that he cares about the woman's good opinion of him and wants to maintain a positive relationship with her.
	• He tries to maintain his dignity and positive self-regard by not showing weakness or insecure feelings.
	• In some cases, he may use it to express good intentions.

What's wrong with it?	• The speaker doesn't admit to any wrongdoing.
	• He shows that he might believe he has done something wrong but doesn't know what. If that's the case, he lacks the courage or common sense to ask.
	• He shows that, if he does know what he did wrong, he lacks the integrity to admit it to her.
	• He doesn't take the time to ask her what she thought and felt about whatever he did, and then listen to her perspective.
	• He doesn't offer a plan for making things up to her, or for ensuring that it won't happen again. No lesson learned.
	• The apology is Self-focused and self-centered, making her feel left out.
How the man sees himself:	A good guy who cares about the feelings of others while retaining his sense of strength and dignity.
How the woman sees him:	A man who is trying to do damage control without admitting that any damage was done; one who may be pretending that he didn't do anything wrong; one who is more concerned with projecting a positive image than with finding out how she feels about his behavior, helping her feel better, or learning from the experience.

The Vague *Apology*

The *Vague* Apology is apologetic in tone and admits wrongdoing or ineptness. However, the speaker doesn't apologize for anything specific.

Examples:

- ♦ "I'm sorry for the way I handled things."
- ♦ "I apologize for anything I said that offended you."
- ♦ "I know I goofed up here, and I'm really sorry."

<table>
<tr>
<td>What's right about it?</td>
<td>

- ♦ The speaker admits to wrongdoing and expresses his regret out loud.
- ♦ He shows that he cares about the woman's opinion of him and wants to maintain a positive relationship with her.
- ♦ He tries to maintain his dignity and positive self-regard by being honest and forthright.
- ♦ He'll get the woman's sympathy, if not her admiration.
- ♦ If this is part of a longer conversation in which he later identifies exactly what he did wrong, then this is no longer a *Vague* Apology and might be part of a successful one.

</td>
</tr>
</table>

What's wrong with it?	• By itself, it lacks a clear indication that the speaker knows exactly what he did wrong, which to her looks weak.
	• He fails to invite her to express her thoughts and feelings on the subject.
	• He fails to propose a plan for making things up to her, if this is appropriate to the situation.
	• Without identifying exactly what he did or said that the woman found hurtful or saw as inept, he will likely repeat his behavior in the future. No lesson learned.
How the man sees himself:	A good guy who is willing to admit to his limitations and say he's sorry.
How the woman sees him:	A man who is trying to do damage control without assessing the damage; a good guy who is somewhat incompetent or clueless and doesn't seem to be motivated to learn from the experience; not bad but also not great; somebody who will likely goof up again.

The Poor Me *Apology*

The *Poor Me* Apology is apologetic in word and tone. However, it's incomplete because it doesn't reflect any lessons learned or finish the job of helping the woman feel better. The speaker deprives the woman of the positive attention she needs as part of her healing process, and instead begs her to pay attention to him so that she can *rescue him* from *his* bad feelings.

Examples:

- "I lost my temper again. I'm so sorry. I feel so bad. I didn't mean it. I always mess up! What's wrong with me?!? *HELP!*"
- "I can see that the story I told sounded stupid and awkward. So sorry, I didn't mean to make you look bad in public, really I didn't. I feel like such an idiot! Please, won't you forgive me?"
- "I always drink too much at these events, don't I? You know I don't do it to hurt you! I really love you and I didn't mean to embarrass you. You have no idea how sorry I am. Please, won't you give me another chance?"

What's right about it?	
	• The speaker admits to specific behavior for which he is truly sorry.
	• He shows that he's aware of causing injury or harm to her, that it's serious, and that he cares about the consequences.
	• He explains that, although he may not know how to change his bad behavior, he wasn't trying to do harm.
	• He accepts full responsibility for his behavior.

What's wrong with it?	• The speaker sounds weak, needy, and undignified.
	• He fails to invite her to express her thoughts and feelings.
	• His attitude is self-centered; in effect, he asks her to help him feel better rather than trying to help her feel better.
	• He doesn't offer any way of making things up to her.
	• He doesn't understand his own motivations well enough to avoid making the same mistake in the future.
	• He doesn't reveal a plan for seeking outside resources to master his problematic impulses.

How the man sees himself:	Deeply sorry, taking full responsibility, being honest, and proving what a good guy he is by apologizing so fully.

How the woman sees him:	A good guy, but one who is weak and groveling as well as draining, exhausting, and burdensome; someone she could pity but not admire; someone she may feel obliged to nurture and help. She may feel sympathetic, but she also feels cheated out of receiving his sympathy and being the focus of his healing attention. Also, unless he learns how to stop his offensive behavior, she could eventually lose sympathy for him.

OVER-APOLOGIES

Over-apologies – apologies that are excessive – are for the most part annoying. They usually indicate that a person is trying too hard to accommodate others and may have adopted a one-down social position. Some over-apologies are bad habits of speech and thought; others signal more complex confusion. Although in some cultures it may be true that women tend to over-apologize more often than men, for the purposes of this chapter the man is shown as the one over-apologizing to the woman.

Except in the special case of *Exaggerated* Apologies that are delivered in a spirit of gentle concern or impish humor, over-apologies are not useful models to emulate. Still, becoming aware of these typical apologies and knowing how to identify them can help you deepen your understanding of yourself and others. When you gain a deeper understanding of yourself and others, it will help you lead more effectively.

The over-apologies in this section are the *Exaggerated* Apology, the *Habitual* Apology, and the *Mistaken* Apology.

The Exaggerated *Apology*

The *Exaggerated* Apology is out of proportion to the situation. It could make the listener either worry about what's wrong with the speaker or wonder whether the speaker is being insincere, flattering her with so much attention. Or, it could make the listener laugh, if there's an appropriate sense of concern and humor in the delivery. For a humorous delivery, imagine the examples below being delivered tongue-in-cheek. For the nervous or frightened delivery, imagine the character of Jerry Lewis.

Examples:

- ◆ "Oh, my! I am SO SORRY!" (An overly dramatic response to a completely inconsequential mistake.)
- ◆ "You mean I gave you *three* ice cubes instead of *two* in your drink!!? How could I have been so *careless*?? Please, won't you forgive me? I promise I'll never, ever do it again!"
- ◆ "I guess you wouldn't know this, but I had peas for lunch today. Your pea soup smells delicious, darling, and I do apologize, but I'll just have to pass on it tonight. I do hope that doesn't hurt your feelings, does it?"

What's right about it?	◆ It can sometimes be an effective apology, if done in good humor and with true consideration for the woman's feelings.
	◆ The speaker may be exaggerating to handle a woman's fears or bad feelings with his gentle sense of humor.
	◆ The speaker may be exaggerating to entertain a woman who enjoys it and plays along.

What's wrong with it?	♦ If the man is afraid that the woman will be angry about an inconsequential offense or a non-offense, then this kind of apology reflects his lack of courage and makes him sound weak.
	♦ Catering to her excessive or inexplicable anger would only fuel her negativity. Consequently, she may use his apology against him in the future regardless of having no right to do so.
	♦ A man who apologizes out of fear to a woman who is unduly angry misses the opportunity to stand up for himself, be strong and honest, and lead her to mature.
How the man sees himself:	The speaker may see himself as trying to dance around a woman's feelings, which he thinks are unreasonable but which he doesn't know how to handle through strong positive leadership. Or, the speaker may see himself as charming and diplomatic or as a comedian or clown.
How the woman sees him:	The woman may see the man as subservient and weak; or as charming, kind, and diplomatic; or as a comedian or clown.

The Habitual *Apology*

The *Habitual* Apology is an apologetic phrase used too frequently, without any apparent thought behind it. It's a strategy for dealing with a large number of social situations in which a brief apology is sometimes appropriate, sometimes not.

Examples:

- "I'm sorry. I'm sorry. I'm sorry." (etc.)
- "Excuse me. Pardon me. Sorry. Excuse me." (etc.)

What's right about it?	• In some situations, saying "I'm sorry" or a similar phrase reflexively is appropriate and desirable.
What's wrong with it?	• When used too often, without any apparent thought behind it, these phrases draw attention to the speaker's lack of common sense in social situations, or the speaker's nervousness or fearfulness. Generally, it makes the speaker seem socially weak.
How the man sees himself:	A nice, responsible man. He may feel that he's getting social points for his apologetic demeanor.
How the woman sees him:	A nice but needy man who needs to be taken care of and mothered – or else a foolish man that she can control and manipulate. If she is motherly, she may see the attention he gets from continually acting sorry as a burden, since it places the burden on her to constantly forgive him so that she can help him feel better about himself. Or, if she's self-serving, she may see his self-effacing attitude as a benefit to her, since by showing weakness he would give her the power advantage in the relationship.

The Mistaken *Apology*

The *Mistaken* Apology is an apology for something outside one's ability to control, or an apology for an imagined offense that wasn't an offense.

Examples:

- "I'm sorry! I didn't mean to embarrass you!" [You didn't! You did just fine.]
- "I apologize for getting sick right when we were going to go to the movies." [If you want to be sorry we missed the movie, fine. But you shouldn't have to apologize for getting sick. That's weak.]
- "It's my fault. I should've chosen a restaurant you'd like more." [How would you know in advance that I wouldn't like the restaurant you chose?]

What's right about it?	- It shows that he has a desire to be responsible and caring.
What's wrong with it?	- It leaves the speaker looking confused, weak, and fearful. - Its inappropriateness may signal a serious problem in the speaker's ability to understand his responsibilities in the relationship. - Unless the listener is extremely self-serving, it makes the listener feel uncomfortable.
How the man sees himself:	A man who wants to do and say the right thing but who feels confused about how to do it.
How the woman sees him:	A nice but needy man who needs to be mothered and helped out of his confusion – or else a foolish man whom she can easily control and manipulate. It either places the burden on her to explain to him what's true and what's not, or it offers her a chance to mess with his mind and confuse him further.

NON-APOLOGIES

A non-apology has the superficial sound of an apology but isn't one at all. Some non-apologies serve to gloss over hard feelings without reference to the cause of those feelings. Others express regret but deny any wrongdoing. Still others are designed to deliver a blow in a war of words.

When a couple argues passionately and both parties become overwhelmed by the constant crisis of the Self gone negative, a non-apology might occasionally slip out. Sometimes this occurs more out of stress and self-defensiveness than a will to inflict harm. At other times, the non-apology is a premeditated strategy: a trick that sets the woman up for a slam, or a technique for maintaining a power advantage in the relationship.

On the other hand, the first two non-apologies shown, the *Forgive and Forget* and the *Sorry, but . . .* Non-Apologies, may in some situations be tolerable conversational statements. On the following pages where these non-apologies are described, you'll learn how.

The non-apologies listed in this section are important to understand so that you can avoid using them (as apologies) in a close personal relationship with a woman – unless you want the relationship to be nothing but a distant memory or a present-day power struggle. They're also provided so that you can call someone out if she should use any of these lines on you.

The non-apologies described in this section are the *Forgive and Forget* Non-Apology, the *Sorry, but . . .* Non-Apology, the *Get Over It* Non-Apology, the *Rusty Nail* Non-Apology, and the *Trickster* Non-Apology.

At the end of this section, one other type of non-apology is discussed, one that is sometimes very appropriate: the refusal to apologize. Refusing to apologize is highly recommended whenever you've done nothing wrong, or whenever you feel no regret for your words or actions. On the other hand, it isn't recommended when your refusal can be used against you with some degree of justification.

The Forgive and Forget *Non-Apology*

The *Forgive and Forget* Non-Apology skips the difficulty of a sincere apology because it doesn't admit wrongdoing, specify what went wrong, or express regret, although it could potentially be delivered sympathetically. It basically appeals to the woman to heal herself rather than providing a healing for her.

When meeting up with an "ex" or former friend, one of these lines might help you deliver sincere good wishes from a distance. However, depending on the way you deliver it, a woman might still hold it against you. Either way, using this type of line could only potentially be useful if you do *not* want to have a close relationship with the person ever again.

Examples:

+ "Let's just forgive and forget."
+ "It's all water under the bridge."
+ "Let's let bygones be bygones."
+ "We made mistakes, but that's all in the past. Let's not go there."

What's right about it?	
	+ The speaker is honest in acknowledging that there were problems in the past in this relationship.
	+ Through body language, facial expression, and vocal inflection, the speaker may demonstrate emotional honesty, possibly including sympathy or regret and even acceptance of some responsibility.
	+ He may be able to create a positive mood for the brief time they are together.
	+ If the relationship is definitely over and isn't worth resurrecting, this non-apology may be a somewhat satisfactory way of expressing good will from a distance.

What's wrong with it?	• The speaker doesn't refer to any specific problems and doesn't articulate any specifics of an apology. • He doesn't admit responsibility for wrongdoing. • It may be a control technique that blocks her from speaking her mind. • It may be a sign that he is fearful and too cowardly to deal with the real issues. • It may be a form of rejection, a way of saying: "You're not worth the time (or our relationship isn't worth the time) it would take for us to have to actually talk about what each of us did to one another, let alone admit responsibility or make amends. I'm not interested in growing with you."
How the man sees himself:	A wise and gracious man, if it's an appropriate expression of good will in a relationship that's definitely over by mutual consent, – OR – Socially clever in avoiding difficult issues.
How the woman sees him:	A wise and gracious man, if it's an appropriate expression of good will in a relationship that's definitely over by mutual consent. – OR – Controlling (if his words may seem to stop her from talking about her thoughts and feelings); cold, dismissive, and uncaring (if that comes across non-verbally); and cowardly, stubborn, and inadequate because unwilling to admit fault or even try to deal with the real issues.

The Sorry, but... *Non-Apology*

The *Sorry, but...* Non-Apology begins with an expression of regret, but then moves into shifting blame to circumstances or to another person. This kind of non-apology often comes up when the speaker has behaved reactively.

In the context of a frank discussion where both parties may be partially at fault, the *Sorry, but...* Non-Apology might sometimes be considered an honest statement and a reasonable starting point. As long as the discussion continues, this kind of statement could be useful in leading to an effective apology once the speaker understands and accepts full responsibility for his behavior. On the other hand, some women find any sort of *Sorry, but...* statement to be offensive at any time.

Examples:

- ◆ "Sorry about that, but I only did it because you made me mad."
- ◆ "I regret what I said. However, it wasn't my fault; I was just answering your question."
- ◆ "Sorry, but I really couldn't resist. That's just my nature."

What's right about it?	
	◆ The speaker acknowledges that he did or said something wrong and expresses sorrow or regret.
	◆ The speaker tries to think through the situation and come up with an explanation based on his understanding of cause and effect.
	◆ The speaker may be trying to come up with a way of preventing the same type of situation from recurring.

What's wrong with it?	♦ The speaker doesn't take full responsibility for his actions.
	♦ The speaker assigns blame to someone or something else rather than focusing on what he could and should have done differently.
	♦ The speaker isn't ready to apologize because he presents himself as weak.
	♦ The speaker doesn't put forth a plan for how he'll avoid the same problem in the future. Instead, he tries to persuade others to change his environment so that he won't be put into a position of making the same mistake again. He might also be trying to ensure that he won't be blamed when he repeats his bad behavior.
How the man sees himself:	An honest man and a logical thinker.
How the woman sees him:	A man who doesn't take responsibility for his actions and who makes excuses.

The Get Over It *Non-Apology*

The *Get Over It* Non-Apology provides a minimal amount of apology-like words but lacks sympathy, or the degree of sympathy necessary for a sincere apology. The man who uses the *Get Over It* Non-Apology with a woman aggressively blames her for expressing the bad feelings he caused her, and instead tries to convince her that, in fact, *he* is the victim of her unreasonable demand for his sympathy. He takes the position that she's hurting him by wanting a satisfying apology from him, since she's essentially asking to be the focus of his attention in a way that doesn't flatter him.

Examples:

- "Of *course* I'm sorry. I'm human and I made mistakes. Do we have to keep talking about this?!"
- "Oh, don't be so hard-hearted. I apologize. Can't you forgive me?"
- "All right, I'm sorry already! Why do you have to take things so hard? Where's your sense of humor? How sad . . . you seem to have lost it."
- "I said I'm sorry! Isn't that enough! Stop dwelling on the past. Can't you just grow up and get over it?!"
- "Don't you think I know what I did? Yes, I'm sorry. Do we have to discuss it again? How do you think it makes *me* feel when you make such a big deal about it? Stop criticizing me! You're impossible."

What's right about it?	• The speaker admits or implies that he did or said something wrong, and offers an acknowledgement, apologetic words, or a statement of regret for doing so. • He tries to handle the problem conversationally while maintaining his strength and power in the relationship.
What's wrong with it?	• The speaker uses a tone of self-pity, harsh judgments, and insults to change the subject or end the discussion. • He devalues the woman by refusing to care for her feelings, thus negating the spirit of an apology.

What's wrong with it? (cont'd.)	◆ He's really saying: "I have no intention of sympathizing with you, and you're bad or wrong for trying to make me. In fact, you should feel sorry for me!"
	◆ He fails to satisfy the woman's emotional needs, which he could only do by listening to her thoughts and feelings and then expressing concern for her.
	◆ He lacks a plan for making things up to her or for avoiding the same mistake in the future.
	◆ He is self-centered, self-pitying, and negatively Other-focused.
How the man sees himself:	◆ If sincere, he feels like a victim – a man who is too harshly punished for what he thinks are relatively minor mistakes.
	◆ If insincere, he feels clever and strong: clever because he's outfoxing her by trying to elicit *her* sympathy rather than offering *his* sympathy, and strong because he's maintaining his power advantage over her by staying in control and essentially trying to make her shut up.
How the woman sees him:	◆ She may see him as a desperate, enraged, belligerent, and thoroughly stressed out man who has lost self-control and needs to get a hold of himself – someone she needs to control and perhaps later to help.
	◆ Or, she may see him as a "Peter Pan" who refuses to grow up and has developed a life strategy of using tricks to outwit others to get what he wants[28] – someone who she feels needs to be told off and taught a moral lesson.
	◆ Or, she may see him as a "Captain Hook," a bully who has enough power over her to "slash her with his hook" or make her "walk the plank" if she doesn't do his bidding[29] – someone she wants to punish and escape.

The Rusty Nail *Non-Apology*

The *Rusty Nail* Non-Apology starts out sounding as if it will be an apology, but by the end of the sentence it becomes a pointed insult. It inflicts a sharp new wound intended to cause lasting pain and anguish, like a rusty nail that punctures the skin and causes tetanus.

Examples:

- "I'm sorry *you feel* that way."
- "I'm sorry you did that to me...."
- "I'm sorry you're such a *bitch*!"
- "I would apologize, but I know you're incapable of forgiveness."
- "I really regret wasting all this time on you."

What's right about it?	• It provides the speaker with a sense of power. • It gives the speaker an opportunity to feel good about himself – at least for the moment.
What's wrong with it?	• Not only is it not an apology; it's an act of aggression that requires an apology. • The speaker fails to admit responsibility for any mistake or to show concern for the woman's feelings. • The speaker devalues the woman. • The speaker feels good about himself by inflicting new pain, which means his non-apology could easily be used against him then *and* in the future. • This kind of tactic will deteriorate the quality of the relationship and could help to end it.

How the man sees himself:	◆ Victorious, temporarily elated, empowered by a strong surge of self-righteousness. In the midst of battle, he has struck a blow and feels like the winner – for the moment.
How the woman sees him:	◆ She may seem him as a desperate, enraged, belligerent, and thoroughly stressed out man who has lost self-control and needs to get a hold of himself – someone she needs to control and perhaps later to help.
	◆ Or, she may see him as a "Peter Pan" who refuses to grow up and has developed a life strategy of using tricks to outwit others to get what he wants – someone who she feels needs to be told off and taught a moral lesson.
	◆ Or, she may see him as a "Captain Hook," a bully who has enough power over her to "slash her with his hook" or make her "walk the plank" if she doesn't do his bidding – someone she wants to punish and escape.

The Trickster *Non-Apology*

The *Trickster* Non-Apology uses apologetic language and is often delivered with dramatic flair, but without any sincerity. It is a total lie fabricated to fool the listener.

Examples:

- ♦ "I'm sorry." (Sorry you caught me, that is!)
- ♦ "I didn't mean to hurt you." (Ha ha, yes I did! I'm a man, and I'll show you who's the boss!)
- ♦ "I would never cheat on you! You know that, don't you?" (You fool, I'm cheating on you now, and I'm cheating on the woman I'm cheating with, too!)
- ♦ "Oh, don't cry, dear. I'm so sorry I hurt you. You're so sweet and beautiful, I would never hurt you intentionally – you know that, don't you?" (Women are so stupid! They'll believe anything as long as you flatter them!)
- ♦ "Sorry. I didn't mean anything by it when I was flirting with her. You're the only one for me, baby!" (...until next week!)

| What's right about it? | ♦ The words sound about right, if only they were true. |
| | ♦ There may be an honest desire to spare the woman from the painful truth of how little he really thinks of her. |

172

What's wrong with it?	◆ It's empty rhetoric that reflects the speaker's lack of integrity.
	◆ It disrespects women.
	◆ If/when discovered, he will lose credibility with her.
	◆ If/when she begins to figure out his game, his apology could easily be used against him.
	◆ He might cultivate an enraged enemy who will seek revenge.
How the man sees himself:	◆ Powerful, clever, and sophisticated
	◆ Smart enough to beat the system and take advantage of others, to have his woman whenever he wants her without having to share his honest inner perspective with her
How the woman sees him:	◆ As long as she's fooled, she may have stars in her eyes and see him as wonderful.
	◆ If she realizes what he's up to, she'll see him as a cunning liar and a manipulative con-artist. In some cases she'll perceive him as a sociopathic womanizer: a man who thinks love is just a game of wits and who therefore lacks a conscience when it comes to deceiving and hurting women. In other cases she may observe that he believes women are morally inferior and should be punished for being that way.
	◆ If she confronts him, she'll see that he's a "Captain Hook," a bully who has enough power over her to "slash her with his hook" or make her "walk the plank" if she doesn't do his bidding – someone she wants to punish and escape.

The Refusal to Apologize

What should you do when you're in a relationship with a woman who thinks you've done something wrong or hurtful, but you strongly believe you haven't . . . and when even after you've explained your point of view clearly and believe that your explanation makes perfect sense, she's still mad and won't back down?

Logically, you can do one of two things: either go ahead and say you're sorry or whatever nonsense she wants you to say (even though in your opinion you did nothing wrong) and then try to move on, or else stand your ground and refuse to apologize.

Here's the dilemma: If you apologize for something you don't really regret because you don't think it was wrong, you're allowing yourself to be controlled and manipulated by a woman, and in the process you're giving up some of your strength as a man. You may see yourself as a clever trickster, but in reality you're cooperating with *her* agenda. This will leave you with residual resentment that won't go away, even if you continually remind yourself that she's the one who's wrong. Also, whenever you humor her, you unconsciously send the vibe that she's mentally or morally less than you are. Even if she believes your pretended apology at the time, in a long-term relationship she will eventually see that you think she's less than you are. She will likely resent this and get even at some point. On the other hand, if you stand up for yourself when she demands that you back down and apologize, you'll probably have a big argument on your hands. Unless the argument results in deeper understanding, she might walk away pouting, try to get even with you then or later, or even break up with you.

This may seem like a no-win situation. Yet if you're sure you don't owe an apology, two winning strategies will help you stay strong while potentially strengthening the relationship.

The first winning strategy is to *turn the conflict into a teaching opportunity*. Instead of pitting your views against her views in an argument, take a counseling role. Just as you would do if you were planning to apologize, find a way to see her in a sympathetic light as you encourage her to talk about all her thoughts and feelings on the topic. Keep listening until you've detected the inconsistencies in her reasoning. Then help her – in a nice way, of course – to see that *her own views don't match up with each other*. If you do this with compassion, a gentle sense of humor, and without blame, she may be able to mature and realize that you were right not to apologize. She would then view you as wise and loving. Not only would you win the argument, but by helping her grow you'd win her admiration. When you stand up for your principles and refuse to compromise your truths, and when you act like an understanding, caring person and give her a chance to talk until you can help her grow and learn, you establish yourself as her leader. If she matures under your leadership, she'll admire you for it. If she can't or won't mature, then move on to the second winning strategy.

The second winning strategy is to *lay down the law*. This means informing her of the rules you live by and letting her know that she needs to live by them too if she wants to continue her relationship with you. Of course, you have to choose laws or rules that you are totally committed to, because if you set a rule for her and then break it yourself, she'll call you out and get the upper hand, and rightly so. Rules or laws to impose on the relationship may include:

- Playing fair
- Being truthful
- Respecting each other's independence
- Acting like adults
- Taking responsibility and admitting mistakes

Let's say that she wants you to apologize for going places without reporting to her where you're going, but you feel that respecting each other's adult independence is one of the rules you intend to live by. You might approach the subject by using the "sandwich principle": (A) State something positive about her point of view first, like the piece of bread at the bottom of the sandwich. Then (B) layer on the contents of the sandwich: your self-affirming statements, your beliefs, and your rule(s). Next, (C) express your positive desire for her cooperation, like the piece of bread that covers the sandwich. Finally, (D) ask her if she'd like a bite of your sandwich or if she wants to take a pass.

(A) "You have every right to your opinions and your feelings. And I respect your feelings and your fears.

(B) "Of course, I have a right to my thoughts and feelings, too, and I feel differently. For me, it's important to maintain my sense of independence, which means I don't want to report my every move to you. I think that would be undignified.

(C) "I love you and I want you to learn to trust me. If you learn to trust me, you shouldn't have to worry about where I am all the time when I'm out. Also, for you, learning to trust will help you overcome your fearfulness.

(D) "Is that something you're willing to try?"

If she's willing to try to trust you and to live by your rule about independence – and if you really are trustworthy – you'll both have new clarity about the parameters of your relationship in a way that won't be used against you in the future. This is your chance to build your leadership and teaching skills, while for her, it's a chance to mature under your leadership guidance. That way, you both win. But even a break-up could be a win for you, since all you would have lost is a relationship with a woman who wouldn't or couldn't mature and who refused to try to trust you.

To reiterate: for any rule you establish, your woman will be watching to see whether you follow the same rule. For instance, if you won't tell her your whereabouts when you're away, she may not want to tell you where she goes when she's away from you, either. As a strong positive leader, you have to live by the rules you set for others. Of course, you don't have to be a strong positive leader, but if you're not, she'll admire you less and use your inconsistencies against you.

Reversing Your Decision

After listening to her for a while, you might realize she made some valid points that you didn't consider earlier in the conversation. For instance, you might discover that you're not sorry for something you said, but maybe you're sorry for the way you said it and the effect it had on her. Or maybe you discover that what she thought you said was not what you thought you said, in which case you could apologize for not expressing yourself more clearly. Maybe you're not sorry for what you did, but you might still be sorry for not letting her know in advance that you were going to do it, since not giving her advance notice caused her some kind of problem.

Whatever the situation may be, if you decide that some type of an apology is called for after all, you can still emerge as a strong positive leader and a winner by following your conscience. Far from appearing weak, changing your mind (if in fact you've changed your mind for a sound and sensible reason) will make you seem mentally and morally strong from a woman's perspective. Conversely, if she walks away thinking that, logically, you should have changed your mind and apologized but were too stubborn or immature to do so, she'll view you as mentally or morally weak, no matter how firmly you may clench your muscles to appear strong when refusing to change your mind.

Reasons for Resistance

What happens when you know you've made a mistake or done something objectionable, and yet you just can't bring yourself to apologize to your woman? Should you force yourself to apologize anyway because some voice in your head says you should, in spite of how wrong it would feel to do so?

Even when you're in the wrong, there are still some situations in which it's defensible to avoid apologizing, at least temporarily. For example, you may decide not to bother apologizing for some mistake because you feel sure that your woman would take it to mean that she was superior to you. In a situation like this, you shouldn't apologize yet because you obviously have a lot of bad feelings that affect your sense of your own value as well as affecting the way you value her.

Such relationships turn the act of apologizing into a game of winners and losers rather than an opportunity for leadership and relationship healing. However, if this is a relationship you're committed to, it might be wise to change the subject temporarily and start discussing the more crucial issues you both need to face, such as what you really think of each other and what you really want from each other. An outside resource such as a relationship counselor or a self-help resource might help you work through your issues, whereas an apology for a specific mistake may not be the best way to begin solving your problems if you feel your apology will put you at a serious disadvantage. Even if you apologized very effectively in that instance, your mistake might continue to be held against you in the future until you iron out the power-related issues. On the other hand, an expertly delivered apology, if you can pull together the self-confidence and find a way to sympathize with her when apologizing, might just bring a glimmer of hope to the relationship.

Men resist apologizing for many reasons. Nevertheless, most women interpret a man's refusal to apologize as unloving and devaluing to themselves, and are inclined to use it against him in the future.

Reasons to Stop Resisting

In addition, your refusal to apologize when your woman believes you should, regardless of your rationale for resisting, could be interpreted as evidence that you lack integrity. She will feel disrespected as a woman and angry that you're not being honest with her, which cuts to the core of her need to feel that she's an equal. These thoughts and feelings, in turn, will make her less happy in the relationship, changing her passionate desire for you into passionate anger or smoldering resentment. And if she's not happy in the relationship, then as long as you're together, she will – in the interest of equality and fair play – do whatever she can to make *you* unhappy, too.

Over time, if you never apologize to her at all, she might become hunched over and start mumbling or stop speaking up – in which case you would win, provided your objective is to hold absolute power in a master-servant relationship. Or, she may hold her head up high, wag her finger at you, resist your leadership, and dedicate herself to lecturing and scolding you or arguing with you in an effort to stand up for herself while teaching you moral lessons that she hopes will make you a more loving man. Or, under the assumption that it's fair game to use you for all you're worth, she may fix herself up and step out on you, spend your available credit if you're the breadwinner, and cheat on you as a way of getting even with you for your lack of care and concern toward her feelings, and as a way of punishing you.

Casanova

Here's an example of a man who, in his quest to do the right thing in his relationship with a woman, goes from dishonestly over-apologizing to refusing to apologize. This quote comes from the Web site SoSuave.com. The author, "Giovanni Casanova," writes:

> I once asked my girlfriend to go with me to a formal dinner party. She refused, for various reasons. I told her that was fine, and took another girl instead, as a friend.
>
> She was pissed. I did not think I had done anything wrong, but I apologized profusely. Apologizing just seemed to make her more angry. I apologized again and again, each time more heartwarming, each time making her more and more angry.
>
> I couldn't figure it out, until I actually thought about it and realized what a chump I was. By apologizing, I was admitting that I had done something wrong. If I had kept my mouth shut, left, and let her burn off her own --- steam, she would have been apologizing to ME for getting so upset.
>
> Instead, she held this little incident over my head for the remaining year and a half of our god-awful relationship.
>
> Another time, I said some things about her sister, who was irritating the living --- out of me at the time. My girlfriend got very angry, and I realized that I was out of line. But I didn't apologize. I simply dropped the argument.
>
> She kept up about it though, and finally I pretended to be angry at HER and left.
>
> A couple hours later she was on the phone begging ME to forgive HER....[30]

Oddly, Casanova concludes that it's better for men to apologize only sparingly – about 25% of the time, he suggests – so as not to give the appearance of being a jerk. Rather than question his own pretense and dishonesty in the relationship from the start, he blames himself for being too nice in the past and advises other men to stop apologizing so much, even at times when they think they're at fault.

With a pseudonym like Giovanni Casanova, this man may not want a long-term relationship. However, if he should ever decide to try for a relationship that lasts, the next time around he might consider using the old "honesty ploy" right from the start. If Casanova stood up honestly for himself and explained calmly and patiently why he felt he had done nothing wrong in the dinner party situation, his girlfriend would eventually have had the option of growing up a little bit or else being dumped. Of course, he might have just walked away and let her burn off her steam, as he later decided, but afterwards he would still need to explain his position to her calmly and patiently if he wanted to avoid similar scenes in the future. Then, whether she decided to stay with him or leave, he would have won by standing up for himself honestly and not allowing himself to be manipulated or controlled.

The problem wasn't that Casanova apologized. The problem was that he apologized dishonestly, believing in his heart that he had nothing to apologize for. The problem was that he lacked the courage to stand up for his principles, forgive his girlfriend for being immature at that moment, and give her a chance to see the light and grow up a little without hating her or scolding her for being imperfect and needing to mature.

According to his account, Casanova later told his girlfriend his honest opinion about her sister. Then he decided that his comments were out of line. Yet instead of apologizing honestly according to his own perceptions and his conscience, he pretended to be mad at his girlfriend for getting mad at him. Again, he chose dishonesty. Many men feel it's their right to express their honest opinions privately in the context of a personal relationship, but since Casanova didn't feel good about what he said, or maybe the way he said it, apologizing would have been a stronger move for him. Instead, pretending to be angry was his way of trying to act powerful.

But pretending to be angry in order to look powerful in his relationship implies that, in reality, he lacked a sense of his own power. Had he stood up for his beliefs and values without pretense, and then held his woman to the same rules that he lived by, he could have looked *and* felt strong.

For example, in writing about the dinner party incident, he admitted that his "heartwarming" apology was insincere. How could his apology have been heartwarming when he believed he had done nothing wrong by inviting the other woman? Maybe his girlfriend held the incident against him for the remaining months of their relationship because it was obvious to her that his "heartwarming" apology had the ring of pretense – which to her would have made him look emotionally dishonest and therefore morally weak. Or maybe he was right that she just had a demanding, controlling personality and thought she could control him from the start. Either way, he could have refused to apologize about the dinner party situation, as he later realized – not because apologizing to a woman is weak, but rather, because apologizing when you're not really sorry and have nothing to apologize for is weak. To be powerful, he could have explained to her his rules for exclusivity in terms of their relationship, stood by them confidently, and given her the choice to agree to live by those rules, negotiate certain aspects of the rules, or break up.

In the other situation, when he said something that he later decided was out of line about his girlfriend's sister and then manipulated his girlfriend by refusing to apologize even though he thought he owed it to her, he might instead have apologized for the language he used (or whatever he thought was out of line) but not the opinion he expressed, if it was an honest opinion. If he were to learn the techniques of effective apologizing described in this book, he could have apologized according to his conscience without losing any power whatsoever.

Staying strong and maintaining power in your relationship are good goals. But remember that you can do so ethically or unethically. Ethical leadership involves being truthful. By being dishonest and manipulative, you can become a strong leader, but not a strong positive leader. Instead, you'd be a strong negative leader, sooner or later resented as selfish and dishonest by the woman in your life.

8

TYPICAL APOLOGIES:
PART II

A complete apology handles the issue in question permanently, or as well as possible. Rather than using the mistake or offense – or your attempt to apologize for it – against you in the future, your woman will remember your complete apology as a point in your favor, a reason she admires and desires you.

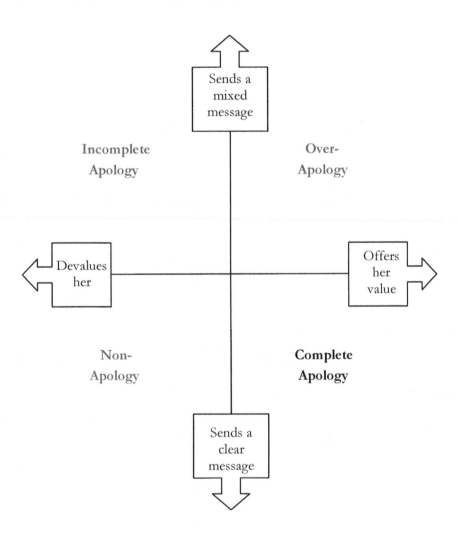

184

Of course, some offenses, such as adultery, are so extreme that an apology alone can't possibly make up for them. These offenses can and will be used against you in the future regardless of the words you select for your apology, at least until you have visibly matured significantly.

In these extreme situations, gaining closure requires that you: 1) offer an apology that's as complete as possible in addressing the issues and that promises behavior changes, and 2) change your behavior for the better, consistent with your promises as a result of personal growth. If your woman accepts your apology and agrees to continue the relationship, your subsequent growth will give you new awareness that will aid you in your ongoing effort to revive at least some of her original relationship dreams. The more you mature, the more she'll remember your apology in retrospect as a first step and an important turning point signifying your increased commitment to loving her.

On the other hand, if you try to change your behavior without any real change in consciousness, your efforts will probably be used against you as soon as your woman figures out your game.

A QUICK REVIEW

In Chapter 3, you learned about the four steps surrounding a successful apology. Chapter 4 presented elements of successful apologies and examples of an apology under two different circumstances, utilizing dimensions of conversation you read about in Chapter 2. Chapters 5 and 6 introduced further information on how to succeed during the apology-related conversation. Chapter 7 offered examples of how not to apologize.

Before learning more about complete apologies in this chapter, let's review the various elements of an apology in the context of the larger process. Remember: the elements you should use at a particular time will depend on the situation and on your woman's personal apology needs and preferences.

- Silently admit to yourself what you did wrong and find a way to feel okay (but not self-righteous) about yourself in spite of your mistake or offense.
- Silently find a way to see your woman in a positive light.
- In a self-accepting and forthright manner, begin the conversation by owning up to your mistake or offense and expressing regret.
- Without making excuses, explain why you think you made the mistake or committed the offense.
- If necessary, initiate a learning-based discussion to get clear on what her issues are, or on other relevant issues (such as your motivations), and if appropriate, end by telling her what you learned.
- Ask her to tell you more about how your words or actions hurt her, listen carefully and sympathetically, and probe until she tells all (so that later, you won't be subjected to further surprises).
- Guide the discussion to get her to reveal something basic that motivates her to be with you, or a relationship dream of hers that she feels was threatened by your mistake or offense.
- Reinforce your desire to make her relationship dreams come true.
- If necessary, use fictional listening.
- If necessary, take breaks and schedule a time to continue the discussion.
- Shower her with appropriate positive attention to help her feel valued again.
- Talk about the consequences of your actions, express sorrow or regret for the grief you caused, and end your statement by focusing on her positive value.
- Propose a plan for making things right, based on reinforcing her key motivation for having a relationship with you. Ask whether she will accept your proposed plan, or ask her to work with you to develop a plan that she will accept.
- Tell her your strategy for utilizing outside resources to help you make the changes you intend to make; follow up by seeking outside resources on your own, so that she doesn't feel she needs to make you do it.
- Reflect on your mistakes, develop a more mature outlook if needed, and follow the apology with appropriate behavior change.
- Seek her forgiveness, verbally or non-verbally.

The Issue of Forgiveness

Part of the age-old formula for apologizing involves asking for forgiveness from the person you hurt or offended. Some would argue that unless you ask the woman for forgiveness, she might hold on to her anger, whereas if the woman says she forgives you, then she'll have no right to hold the issue against you in the future. In the real world, though, if she's still angry somewhere inside, your woman *will* bring it up again, regardless of whether she said at the time that she would forgive you. Sometimes saying, "I forgive you" – or for that matter, "I'm sorry" – can be nothing more than a word game, a verbal ritual that fools one or both parties into a false sense that no bad feelings lurk beneath the surface. If she says, "I forgive you" when she still feels some anger, it may be a trick on her part, but it's more likely that she doesn't fully realize at the time just how bad she still feels. Either way, her "I forgive you" won't stop her from using your mistake or offense or flawed apology against you in the future.

Of course, forgiveness is what you need and want. But is asking for it the best way to get it? Or is there a better way?

My view is that often, asking for forgiveness after you've offended or hurt a woman is like asking her to do you a favor right after you've taken something away from her. Asking her for forgiveness can sometimes be a way of asking her to help you feel better, rather than a way for you to take care of her. If you've done something that hurt or offended your woman, she'll think it's *her* turn to be taken care of, not her job to take care of your bad feelings about yourself right after you've devalued her.

On the other hand, some women specifically want to be asked for forgiveness. If your woman feels this way, it's only right to respect her feelings by doing so. Asking for forgiveness makes you vulnerable and gives your woman the power to accept or reject you. She may appreciate you showing your vulnerability and find that quality endearing.

Unfortunately, showing your vulnerability by asking for forgiveness can backfire if she still feels devalued at the time you ask for it. In that case, asking her to forgive you will give her the ability to use her power against you to get even – making herself feel better at your expense, not because of your help. This will temporarily relieve her hurt feelings without solving the problem of mending your relationship and will undercut your attempt to heal her. In this situation, she's likely to continue the conflict and possibly use your apology against you.

By contrast, if you help her feel valued again through your positive words and behavior, she'll have little reason to hold power over you. That is, start using your leadership power *wisely* and she'll enjoy, appreciate, and desire you for your powerfulness, rather than trying to take power away from you to get even for her hurt feelings.

Finally, if you follow the four steps surrounding the effective apology from Chapter 3, you'll find that forgiveness is often likely to occur non-verbally.

COMPLETE APOLOGIES

There are two types of complete apologies. The *Gentleman's* Apology is the one to use when your mistake or offense was unintentional. This kind of apology can turn an awkward situation into an opportunity to score acceptance and admiration from your woman – and from anyone else who might be witnessing your delivery. Whether it's a quick apology for a simple mistake or part of a lengthy conversation about a more serious offense, apologizing like a gentleman ultimately leaves you with the halo effect.

At other times, when the hurt you caused your woman was intentional or partly intentional, or when your behavior was out of control, there's a second type of apology called the *Heroic* Apology. By itself, the *Heroic* Apology doesn't handle the issue permanently, or even temporarily. Rather, by being as complete as possible, it can create space in which she might place you on probation rather than expelling you from her life. During your probation, if she offers it to you, you'll get a chance to make a greater commitment to the relationship by backing up your apologetic words with appropriate actions and new attitudes.

If you change your behavior permanently as a result of maturing, she may eventually come to remember your apology as healing. The more she feels valued by your renewed commitment to the relationship and your respectful behavior, the more she'll be able to let herself admire and desire you once again. Apologizing like a hero and then making a heroic self-sacrifice to back it up is a transformative process that leaves you a better man.

These complete apology models take time, energy, practice, and conscious determination to master. However, becoming an expert at both types of complete apologies will enhance your power in your relationship as it wins you your woman's greater respect, admiration, and loyalty. What's more, your private leadership development in the process will likely impact other areas of your life, potentially benefiting your career, social standing, family relationships, and friendships.

The Gentleman's *Apology*

Use a Gentleman's Apology when you made an innocent mistake that caused your woman harm or upset from which she cannot fully recover on her own.

Example 1:

- "Wow, I blew it. I can't believe I forgot our anniversary! I'm sorry. I had it written on my calendar, but I've been so busy at work that I lost track. It wasn't intentional, honey. But you look hurt, and I'm so sorry. You didn't deserve this. Please tell me, how did it make you feel? I want to understand your experience." (Let your woman talk; show concern for her thoughts and feelings; listen respectfully.) "I respect your views, and I'm so sorry for causing you all of those bad feelings. You're such a sweetheart. You really are special to me and you deserve better than this. Please let me make it up to you.
  - Proposal A: "I know the timing is late, but would you like to go for a getaway weekend in two weeks? I'll be done with that project and can focus my attention on you to show you how special you are to me."
  - Or, proposal B: "I really want us to find some time and space so that I can show you just how special you are to me. There must be a way to do it in spite of the limited time and money available. Do you have an idea for how you'd like us to celebrate over the weekend?"

Example 2:

- "Oh, I'm so sorry! Are you okay? Here, let me help you up. I didn't mean to push you over like that! I guess I wasn't looking where I was going. How are you feeling? (Then let her talk as you show concern for her feelings and interest in everything she says.)

- If she's okay: "Oh good, I'm glad you're all right then! Sorry – I'll try to watch where I'm going next time. Are you sure you're okay?"
- OR if very serious: "Oh, wow. Here, let me get a cold pack to stop the swelling." (Offer to take all steps necessary to help her, and continue giving her your undivided attention until she has recovered completely.)

What's right about it?	The man confidently: • Says what happened and expresses regret (without appearing weak or talking about how bad making the mistake makes *him* feel). • Takes full responsibility for his mistake. • Explains why he acted as he did, not to excuse it but to let her know it wasn't intentional. • Finds out the harm caused and expresses sincere regret. • Asks questions to learn her perspective and talks about what he learned from her or from his mistakes. • Focuses appropriate attention on the woman to restore and reinforce her feeling of positive value. • Takes action to make amends or proposes a plan for making amends in the future.
What's wrong with it?	• Nothing, as long as it's appropriate to the situation.
How the man sees himself:	• Humbled, flawed. • Caring, responsible, decent, competent, and gentlemanly.
How the woman sees him:	• Human, flawed. • Caring, responsible, decent, competent, and gentlemanly; someone she would likely trust, admire, respect, and believe in.

Gentleman or Hero?

In America today, the difference between a heroic deed and a good deed is sometimes blurred. Yet being a gentleman isn't the same as being a hero. When a gentleman offers a *Gentleman's* Apology to a lady and it helps her feel better, he is praiseworthy and admirable, yet not really heroic since he doesn't risk any big loss by apologizing. The worst thing that could happen to him would be to have his apology rejected; however, if his mistake was innocent to begin with, her rejection of his apology would ultimately make *her* look bad, not him. Likewise, when a gentleman helps an elderly lady cross the street, he is praiseworthy but not really heroic. Even if he helps the lady survive by doing so, he doesn't take any significant personal risks in the process.

Heroes, on the other hand, behave selflessly and bravely by taking a major risk in the process of helping or saving someone else or some group of people – like the firefighter who enters a burning building to rescue someone trapped inside, or the soldier who goes to battle for his country.

Of course, heroes deserve great honor and praise for their risks and sacrifices. Yet sometimes we praise and honor heroes in a way that makes them seem superhuman, as if they were perfect. Unfortunately, this false perception gives boys and men the idea that, to be a hero, they either need to be nearly perfect or else they should hide their faults and blunders so that the public will believe they're perfect. This incentivizes men to conceal and deny some aspects of themselves, which puts them at greater risk of being humiliated if the world discovers that they're just flawed human beings like the rest of us.

To avoid this predicament, it's a good idea to acknowledge your shortcomings and find a way to feel self-accepting without being self-righteous. Remember that even the great heroes from days gone by – Columbus, Martin Luther King, Jr., Alexander the Great, Napoleon, Gandhi, Socrates, Confucius – were flawed human beings. That's a good thing, because it means that no matter what mistakes you've made, you, too, can become heroic by rising to the occasions that are presented to you.

TYPICAL APOLOGIES: PART II

Hercules

A classic example of a hero is the mythological figure of Hercules. According to mythology scholar Edith Hamilton, Hercules was known throughout ancient Greece as both the "greatest of all heroes" and the "strongest man on earth."[31]

As Hamilton retells the story,[32] Hercules was a sympathetic character but had a hot temper and lacked emotional self-control. Early in his life, when he was married to Princess Megara, he temporarily went mad (due to a spell cast on him) and murdered their three sons before slaying Megara as well. When he later returned to his senses and realized what he had done, he was devastated. He contemplated suicide as the only fair way to punish himself. Luckily, his friend Theseus talked him out of it, saying that suicide would be cowardly and that "men of great soul can bear the blows of heaven and not flinch."[33] In an effort to redeem himself, Hercules performed the famous 12 Labors of Hercules. In these labors, Hercules faced nearly impossible challenges, such as slaying a 9-headed monster called the Hydra. By fighting this monster and performing other tasks of monstrous proportions, he proved that, in spite of his grievous offenses, he was a great man. The ancient Greeks believed that "by his sorrow for wrongdoing and his willingness to do anything to expiate it, he showed greatness of soul."[34]

Apologizing Like a Hero

A *Heroic* Apology is an apology that occurs during a long conversation that you voluntarily enter into because you want to accept responsibility for your out-of-control, extreme, or intentionally malicious behavior. You also want to pay for whatever harm your behavior has caused and reverse the damage if possible in order to redeem yourself. You enter into this conversation knowing that your self-esteem will likely take several hits as you work to rescue your woman's value and achieve heroic stature. If you fail, you have much to lose, including a meaningful relationship and a sense of your own value. But like Hercules, you can redeem yourself if you decide to accept yourself as a flawed but well-meaning man (without being self-righteous about it) and do whatever it takes to make amends. In your case, you'll need to work hard to understand her and then sacrifice selfish aspects of yourself to earn back her trust. By being sorry for your wrongdoing and by doing whatever it takes to make up for it, you can achieve a type of heroic greatness respected by the ancient Greeks.

A *Heroic* Apology is harder to deliver than a *Gentleman's* Apology. In a *Heroic* Apology you not only have to claim full responsibility for your behavior and then refocus on rebuilding your woman's value, but also give up your old identity to some extent and reconstruct your value in a more realistic way than before. Because you were at fault when offending her, you need to be open to learning from within, from your woman, and from outside resources. Finally, to get closure you have to sacrifice an immature aspect of yourself. That self-sacrifice is ultimately what makes you heroic as well as once again desirable to her.

The difficulty of offering a *Heroic* Apology depends on how much hurt you've each inflicted in the past and on how harshly you judge yourself. The longer your relationship has been built on dealing negative blows to one another, the greater a challenge it will be to sort through your issues until you can reconnect to your own value as well as hers. You may face self-doubts, feelings of inadequacy, feelings of being unloved and unappreciated, feelings of shame or humiliation, and other bad feelings that weaken your sense of your own value. You may also have to sort out self-righteous feelings of anger, resentment, contempt, rage, and hatred. These self-righteous feelings make you feel powerful, but unfortunately, they also trap the associated weaker feelings inside you so that you can't overcome them. This blocks your ability to mature, and without maturing further, you'll be incapable of healing your woman or enjoying a successful relationship with her in the future.

By meeting your challenges with manly courage and the intent to be fair, and by accepting your respective imperfections rather than being self-righteous, you can succeed. To voluntarily enter the realm of these feelings requires tremendous courage and a burning desire to be responsible and do something right to redeem yourself – qualities of a true Herculean hero.

Like Hercules, you may have to defeat some "monsters" in your relationship. These "monsters" are forces within you or within her that make you or her seem like a monster. If your woman has felt devalued by you in the past, you might think she looks and sounds like a monster when she starts complaining or reprimanding you. Moreover, if over the years you've felt devalued by her, or by life itself, you may find yourself spiraling out of control at times, as if controlled by monstrous forces within yourself as you try desperately to regain your feelings of power and value. In other words, your feelings could sometimes turn you into a monster, just as her feelings sometimes turn her into a monster.

To get the positive attitudes you need before you can succeed in delivering a *Heroic* Apology, your challenge is to combine your courage and wits to defeat these "monsters" without slaying the imperfect but nevertheless good human beings – yourselves – trapped inside them. This process involves using techniques for pulling yourself out of ICM and for handling feelings – techniques you've learned in previous chapters.

By the end of this learning/apologizing conversation – if you do it well – you'll feel mixed feelings about yourself that will become more positive the more you grow as a result of it. In this case, *growing* involves both a loss (sacrifice) and a gain. What you lose is something that wasn't real in the first place, like conceit and delusional thinking, or self-centered gamesmanship masquerading as intelligence, or misplaced childhood rebellion. What you gain is a better, more mature version of you, like an upgrade. In giving up your self-righteousness you'll suddenly feel weaker, but paradoxically, you'll become a better man, more impressive to others, and more likeable. Gradually, you'll begin to feel a new type of power, the power of integrity, along with a justifiable sense of your own authentic value due to your success in completing your heroic challenge.

Because of the negative or mixed or out-of-control feelings that drove your hurtful behavior, a well-delivered *Heroic* Apology will leave your woman feeling hopeful though not yet healed. Her hope is that, by working together toward mutual understanding, you'll both be happier together as you mature. Her healing and your increased happiness as a couple depend on your long-term follow-through after the apology is over.

The *Heroic* Apology is a critical initial step in a much larger arc of changing bad feelings to good ones in your relationship. Most of that process will be accomplished not by the apology, but by your personal growth following the apology. Over time, your Herculean "labor" can, in her eyes, gradually elevate you from the status of jerk or abuser to the stature of a good man – and in the Herculean sense, a hero.

The Heroic *Apology*

Use a *Heroic* Apology whenever the harm you inflicted was extreme, intentional, or driven by out-of-control emotions.

The first example below is an excerpt of a longer conversation, one that began with your woman complaining emphatically about the fact that you called her a bitch, which you did in response to many other insults and complaints she hurled at you first. Some apology elements have been handled, such as listening to her point of view. This excerpt is also part of the broader on-going conversation of your entire relationship, in which you've both made many accusations and expressed many unhappy feelings.

Example 1:

- ♦ "I called you a bitch, it's true. The way you treated me, it was hard for me to understand what you were feeling. I only knew that you kept getting me to help you around the house and then criticizing the way I did it. You seemed so cruel and unfair to me.

  "But I think I'm beginning to understand what you've been telling me. I'm beginning to get the enormity of your frustration. Now I see that the ways I act in other areas of life, and the ways I've acted in the past, are all connected to the way you feel about me now, and that just helping you with small things around the house doesn't really make up for all the frustration I've caused you by acting like I was so much better than you for so many years.

  "When you told me just now about how bad I've made you feel, it sounded like your frustration on a scale of 1 to 10 is about a 70. Is that about right? [No, it's about 700!] Wow, I am so sorry for causing you that incredible amount of pain! That must be hard for you to deal with. [Yes!] Well, you deserve better. Is there more you'd like to tell me about how I made you feel? (She talks for a while, getting upset again as she talks.) Wow, that sounds like it feels awful. [Yes!]

  "You know, when we first met, I actually thought I was putting my best foot forward to try to impress you, but I'll admit I lied about my background. I'm sorry. I knew that was wrong, but I guess I did it because I saw you as incredibly valuable and I was afraid that you wouldn't have loved me for who I was. I wanted you so much that I pretended to be somebody I thought you would love. Then, when you believed me and looked up to me, I could see that I had you fooled. So I went with it.

"The truth is that, in spite of my worst behavior, I really do love you and I still want you to love me. You're not a bitch. You're a beautiful woman who feels frustrated, lonely, hurt, and disappointed. I guess I called you that to try to control you, and I'm sorry – that was unfair. You don't need to be controlled – you need to be listened to and respected. You deserve better, and I still want to get it right so that I can make you happy.

"I know your frustration limits your ability to have patience with me, and that's understandable. But if I'm going to learn how to be more honest and responsible and fair to you, I need you to accept me as I am or it won't work. I know I've made a lot of mistakes, but I can't feel okay about myself now when you're constantly criticizing me. I would like you to be more patient and accepting so that I can get better at this. Do you think you could do that? [I'll try.]

"We both need to respect each other's limitations so we can be happier together. However, I accept full responsibility for my actions, and I'm sorry. I want to be the man you need me to be. I really love you and want us to get back to the love we started out with – do you? Will you help me figure out how to work on this together?"

Of course, the above apologetic excerpt *could and would be used against you in the future* unless you worked to keep up your end of the bargain for the rest of your relationship. In a *Heroic* Apology, the words alone are never enough. It takes real self-sacrifice through consistent behavior change – a willingness and determination to give up being selfish and immature at her expense – to heal the relationship and help your woman feel valued once again.

Example 2:

The second example of a *Heroic* Apology takes place after an out-of-control philandering man was caught by his long-suffering wife, the mother of his children, after years of cheating. Here the same rules apply: no words can fix this problem, but a *Heroic* Apology followed by the self-sacrifice of giving up his selfish, deceitful, disrespectful behavior and trading it in for mature, responsible, respectful behavior can gradually counteract the hurt she feels. This will help her begin to rebuild a sense of her own value. The conversation picks up after the woman has confronted the man's infidelity and has spent a long time expressing her feelings, perceptions, opinions, and judgments about it.

- ◆ "You have every right to be angry, since I've been cheating on you for so long. I know that if I found out you were cheating on me, I'd be furious, so I understand your feelings to some extent. You're right – this is my fault. We both took a vow. You kept the vow and I broke it.

    "But you've asked me why I did it, and I'm going to try to explain it to you, because you deserve an explanation. This doesn't excuse my behavior, but at the time I had a lot of beliefs that led me to act that way.

    "First, I believed that I was too smart to get caught. I was delusional to think I was that much smarter than you. If I were really smart I would have understood that just about anyone can get caught eventually, especially when they're with a smart woman. Sure, maybe some guys get away with cheating, but they're not necessarily smarter than I am. Maybe they're just with women who are clueless or who turn a blind eye, and you're definitely better than that.

    "Second, I believed the old maxim that 'what you don't know won't hurt you.' What I've learned from you these past weeks is that, even though you didn't technically know what I was up to for a long time, you had a sense all along that something was amiss, and that made you feel devalued. And now, of course, finding out the extent of my bad behavior has devastated you emotionally, which I really regret because you don't deserve that. I never wanted to hurt you. Talk about delusion – I actually thought I could make you happy while making myself and other women happy, too. When I sensed that you weren't happy with me, I blamed you instead of realizing that you sensed more about me than I realized you could. I was wrong to blame you for feeling unhappy. You've always tried your best to love me and you've dedicated your life to me and to raising our children. I only hope that someday I can prove deserving of your devotion.

"Third, I believed that if I played my cards right, I could 'have it all.' What I've learned is that nobody really has it all, and nothing worthwhile is cheap or easy. When a man has a valuable relationship, it's only fair to provide value in return. In return for having the honor of your fidelity I promised you my fidelity, and because I didn't make that sacrifice as a man, I now have to pay an even bigger price in terms of humiliation, and in terms of the hard work it takes now to hopefully earn back your trust and make you happy in the future. And unfortunately, you and the kids have to pay a big price for my behavior. I know this situation has made you very unhappy, and I'm sorry. You're valuable to me and I don't want to lose you. I still hope to be able to make you happy again and to hold our family together by becoming a better man. You deserve my dedication and fidelity. It's only fair, and I want to be a big enough man to give you the love you deserve.

"Fourth, I believed that almost all men cheated, and that to prove my manhood and compete with other men, I had to score as many sexual conquests as possible. The more conquests I could mark on my scorecard, the sexier and manlier and more powerful I felt. Basically, I was more interested in being a stud than in anything or anyone else. I thought all that talk about having integrity and faithfulness was a bunch of empty rhetoric and that real men know it's a joke. However, now that I've been in therapy, I realize that I was discounting a lot of successful men in society who don't cheat, and who hold different standards of manhood. I realize that there's a better class of men and I want to be one of them. One of their main standards for true manhood is self-discipline. Another is having the courage and intelligence to confront a bad situation and work to change it for the better.

"That leads me to the fifth belief I lived by, which is the belief in Nature as the ultimate law, the ultimate truth. When I saw an attractive woman who was available and seemed interested in me, my nature led me to move in for the conquest. I thought it would be foolish not to do what felt natural. But after thinking about it, I now realize that natural instincts can lead people to do all sorts of bad and destructive things, including abuse and murder. That's why self-discipline and constructive action are the true marks of manhood and are superior to blindly following your nature and giving in to temptation.

"The idea that sneaking around to have a lot of sex makes you a real man is laughable. Having a lot of sex in a sneaky way makes you basically an overgrown teenager overwhelmed by his hormones, especially in comparison with the *real* challenges of manhood that include not only being sexual in an appropriate, self-disciplined way but also having the courage, discipline, and intelligence to play fair and still manage to get enough of what you need and want in life.

"It all started when I wasn't getting your undivided attention anymore because you were taking care of the kids. Then I started traveling on the job and being tempted by the attention other women were giving me. I filled my need for attention by giving in to temptation. I thought I could outsmart the system and stay ahead of the game.

"But now I see that I was being extremely self-centered. Whenever I was home, I could have had you arrange for a babysitter so that you and I could go out together more often and give each other attention. On the road, I could have called you more often just to listen sympathetically to the things you wanted to share with me, instead of saying what I wanted and then cutting off the conversation. I could've even helped you around the house when I was home. In other words, I could've done things to give *you* attention and helped you shoulder some of the burdens of our family to *earn* your attention in return. Instead, I felt *entitled* to your attention at all times, even though I wasn't giving you the attention you needed, and even though you were home 24/7 taking care of the kids.

"It would have taken self-discipline for me to resist the temptations around me. But instead I acted like a self-righteous teenager, out to get everything I could without giving back much in return other than resentment and a sense of entitlement.

"So that's about it. There are truly no words to express how sorry I am about my failures and about the grief, humiliation, rage, and devastation I have put you through. I know that our children will someday learn about what their daddy did. Maybe they'll become sexually irresponsible too, since I'm their role model. Or maybe they'll hate me some day for what I did to you, their mother. Maybe both. But what's done is done, and I'll have to meet those challenges later on.

"Right now, I still love you and hope that you'll give me a chance to love you better. And I still care about the kids. I want to be with you so that we can provide them with a stable home life. I want to be a good father and teach them what it means to be a real man giving real love to their mother on a daily basis, even as I work every day to meet the higher standards of manhood.

"I want you to know that I'm committed to us, to our family, and to becoming the man you need me to be. My plan is to continue with my therapy and with our couples therapy. I feel that I need outside resources to ensure that I stay on track and to keep on learning from other men about this new concept of manhood that I really didn't understand before, since my dad never had time to teach me much at all. I want to be a real man, and to do so I know I need to make things right for you. I just hope you'll give me that chance.

"I'm not going to ask you to forgive me because I know that what I've done is unforgivable. Only my behavior change over time can earn your trust. But it's really up to you to decide whether we can move forward together. At this point, would you be willing to let me stay with you so that we can keep working on our relationship together? And will you continue to share your ideas with me about how to do it?"

What's right about it?	• He admits responsibility for specific actions.
	• He recounts his behavior and shows that he understands how his actions have affected others.
	• He expresses sorrow for his actions and their effects.
	• He explains his motivations in a reasoned way and sounds like he's being honest about it.
	• He tells his woman what he's learned.
	• He builds her value by giving her lots of eye contact and referring to her in positive ways.
	• He shows that he has already listened attentively to her perspective and has worked to understand it.
	• He responds sympathetically to her point of view, showing respect and giving her appropriate credit.
	• He proposes a plan for reclaiming their mutual relationship hopes and dreams and asks her whether she will accept and co-create the plan.
	• He shows signs of being willing to sacrifice his selfishness, conceited posturing, and deceitfulness, and to exchange these for a more humble but decent and respectful attitude.
	• He demonstrates that he has already matured by reflecting on his actions and motivations, which bodes well for his promises to change and to continue working to heal the relationship.
	• By continuing to reflect and mature, he positions himself to effect a relationship healing over time.
What's wrong with it?	• Nothing, as long as it's heartfelt and represents a genuine commitment to growth.

How the man sees himself:	A man who:
	• Is humbled by his failure.
	• Realizes that he has been delusional and unfair, and is ready to face himself.
	• Wants to become a better, more loving man.
	• Wants to become responsible and is willing to make changes and do whatever it takes to prove his value.
	• Is basically good, caring, and willing to learn from his mistakes and from others.
	• Is committed to his relationship and to redeeming himself by making a greater commitment to others.
How the woman sees him:	A man who:
	• Has committed a grievous offense that devalued and disrespected her and spoiled her dreams.
	• Seems committed to being responsible and learning to do better.
	• She hopes she can someday trust again, but only if he proves himself through his ongoing actions.
	• Has the capacity to heal her wounds and offers her hope that he will do so.
	• Offers her hope that her dreams of being loved and cared for and of raising a family together may still come true, though in an imperfect way.
	• She hopes to once again admire and desire, if he really changes.

9

AFTER THE APOLOGY

Y ou've done your best and offered your woman an apology. Now you
have to wait and see whether she's going to accept or reject it. Yet if
she says she accepts it, how will you know whether she has really let go of
the issue? And if she rejects your best effort, what do you do next?

APOLOGY ACCEPTED . . . OR NOT

When she accepts your apology, your woman's body language will probably
reveal whether she feels good again or whether she's caving in or possibly
laying a trap. If she's sincere in accepting your apology, and if your apology
was appropriate and complete, she will look as though she has recovered
and is somewhat hopeful or optimistic. However, if her acceptance is half-
hearted and she's caving in just to keep the peace between the two of you,
she might look hunched over, depressed, resigned, or just low in energy.
Then again, if she comes across as extremely polished and high-energy and
accepts your apology too easily, watch out. She may be planning to get even.

As mentioned earlier, one reason a woman rejects a man's apology is
that the man doesn't feel good about himself from the start and spends the
apology trying to restore his own value instead of apologizing from a
position of strength and self-confidence. By forgetting to focus on her inner
experience and compassionately restore her value, he ends up sounding self-
centered and weak.

If your apology is rejected, don't immediately blame yourself, but don't
immediately blame her, either. Begin by assessing your performance:

- Did you apologize mostly to ease your guilt, or to help her feel better?
- Did you honestly feel you owed this apology? If not, she may have
  picked up on your dishonesty.
- Did you apologize for the right thing, or did you misunderstand what
  she's upset about?
- Was your apology appropriate to the situation – neither too much nor
  too little?
- Did you feel valuable when apologizing? Or was it a devaluing
  experience for you? If offering the apology left you feeling devalued,

ask yourself questions to determine when, why, and how you lost a sense of your value.

- Did your apology help her feel valuable or did it appear to make her feel devalued? If she seems to feel devalued by it, you may need to review the big picture of setting up and delivering the apology, or review ways to handle ICM, or review the elements of an effective apology to be sure you included all elements appropriate to your situation.

If you're still not sure what went wrong, ask her for input. She may just want to negotiate the terms of your apology proposal, or talk about another issue she hasn't shared yet. Ask questions to learn what's still needed.

In the process, you might learn that layers of history between the two of you are bringing down her emotions and rendering her unable to hear your apology. If so, you may need to have a longer, deeper conversation. After sorting out your issues, try switching from a *Gentleman's* Apology to a *Heroic* Apology, if appropriate.

If you're sure you're doing everything right in the apology, your woman may be rejecting your efforts in order to gain a power advantage. If you believe this is the case, you should seriously reflect on your own methods of asserting power in the relationship. When a man uses his power wisely in a relationship, behaving like a strong positive leader, his woman generally has no reason to try to take power away from him – unless she's a sociopath. If you suspect that she may be a sociopath, start reading books on the subject immediately to educate yourself. Otherwise, work on developing strong positive leadership skills and becoming less dictatorial – or less passive, as the case may be. That way, there's a good chance you'll be able to garner her admiration for your wise use of power as a leader, rather than inspiring her to compete with you for power.

When a woman feels truly valued by a man who truly values himself during an apology, there's less of a chance of rejection. All elements of an effective apology – including taking responsibility, listening sympathetically, expressing regret, and making amends when possible – relate directly to a man's ability to restore the woman's value and, in the process, prove his own.

207

Following Up

When your apology is accepted, remember to learn from the experience. If you spilled a drink and apologized for it, then be extra careful to avoid spilling a drink again. If you said something rude and apologized for it, be more aware in the future so that you don't repeat that mistake. If you promised to stop belching in public for the fun of it, grow up and stop it. And if she's still interested in you after you've cheated on her, follow up by getting outside help and make a commitment to becoming a better man.

Are you happy now??!?

Offering your woman complete apologies whenever appropriate can raise your woman's level of happiness over time. However, happiness may not be the result of a single effective apology. Patient, consistent effort is the key. If you offer your woman a winning *Gentleman's* Apology, she may walk away smiling because of the extra attention you've given her. Yet even then, doing rude things and apologizing effectively for them is probably not a useful strategy for making your woman happy.

When you make a mistake that hurts your woman's feelings, she feels "not okay." That's negative territory. Then, when you restore her value, she feels okay again. It's like being back to square one. However, square one is neutral, not positive territory, so delivering appropriate, effective apologies will raise her happiness level mostly by making her less unhappy. Yet true happiness feels better than okay. When she feels truly happy, your woman's feelings go from neutral territory to positive territory. Secrets to making your woman feel happy include reinforcing her positive value and providing her with lots of appropriate attention in a balanced way on a regular basis.

That said, if your past attempts to apologize or refusals to apologize have been a source of grief to your woman, you can gradually make a meaningful difference in how happy your woman is to be with you by learning to deliver a complete apology whenever the opportunity arises.

RESTORING VALUE

People generally gain and lose a sense of value by the way they're treated by others over time. That's why famous celebrities, corporate executives, and the popular kids at school can potentially become delusional about how great they are, and why people who as children were seriously bullied at school or mistreated by some teachers or by their parents can lack a sense of their full value as adults. Of course, people can and often do value themselves in spite of their relationships, but this weakens the relationships.

The best love relationships have a positive physical, emotional, mental, and spiritual energy exchange most of the time. Each person feels valued by the other, which affirms and reinforces each one's feelings of being a valuable man or woman.

Why do women bring up old wounds again and again? It's simple: whatever issue or event your woman keeps bringing up caused her to feel that she lost some of her value, and she wants it back. She keeps bringing up the issue or the event to get you to understand her loss so that you can restore her value to where it was before the issue or event occurred. In other words, your woman wants you to rescue some part of her value that she lost because of you and that she can't recover on her own. Once you understand what's needed and restore that part of her value, she will feel better – more valuable, loved, and whole – and will no longer need to bring it up.

Finally, offering a complete apology, when appropriate, can restore your own value as well as hers. When you make a mistake that hurts your woman and you know you've caused her some pain, somewhere inside your mind you probably judge yourself negatively and lose a little bit of your own value. At the same time, she feels robbed of some of her value by whatever you said or did and might turn around and try to devalue you in retaliation. By offering her a complete apology, where you retain your dignity and maintain a sense of power and value while delivering it, you can help her feel better about herself and about you, which will then help you feel better about yourself and about her. This will increase your sense of your own positive influence and general competence. As a result, she will accept, appreciate, admire, and desire you more.

Recommended Resources
and Works Cited

RECOMMENDED RESOURCES AND WORKS CITED

On Apologies

Blanchard, K., & McBride, M. (2003). *The One Minute Apology: A Powerful Way to Make Things Better*. New York: William Morrow/HarperCollins Publishers, Inc.

Bloom, L. (2008). *The Art of the Apology: How to Apologize Effectively to Practically Anyone*. Green Angel Media, LLC.

Casanova, G., & DeepBlue. What Happens When You Apologize to a Woman. Retrieved from www.sosuave.com/halloffame/hall259.htm (Accessed 3/8/2009)

Chapman, G., & Thomas, J. (2006). *The Five Languages of Apology: How to Experience Healing in All Your Relationships*. Chicago: Northfield Publishing.

Engel, B. (2001). *The Power of Apology: Healing Steps to Transform All Your Relationships*. New York: John Wiley & Sons, Inc.

Griswold, C. (2007). *Forgiveness: A Philosophical Exploration*. New York: Cambridge University Press.

Kador, J. (2009). *Effective Apology: mending fences, building bridges, and restoring trust*. San Francisco: Berrett-Koehler Publishers, Inc.

Lazare, A. (2004). *On Apology*. New York: Oxford University Press, Inc.

Smith, N. (2008). *I Was Wrong: The Meanings of Apologies*. New York: Cambridge University Press.

Tavuchis, N. (1991). *Mea Culpa: A Sociology of Apology and Reconciliation*. Stanford, CA: Stanford University Press.

On Leadership and Influence

Carnegie, D. (1936). *How to Win Friends & Influence People*. New York: Simon and Schuster. Page references are to the 1998 Pocket Books edition.

Coffman, C., & Gonzalez-Molina, G. (2002). *Follow This Path: How the World's Greatest Organizations Drive Growth by Unleashing Human Potential*. New York: Warner Books, Inc.

Covey, S. (1989). *The Seven Habits of Highly Effective People: Restoring the Character Ethic*. New York: Simon and Schuster.

On Masculinity and Heroism

Belushi, J. (2006). *Real Men Don't Apologize*. New York: Hyperion.

Bly, R. (1990). *Iron John: A Book About Men*. Reading, MA: Addison-Wesley Publishing Company, Inc.

Hamilton, E. (1940). *Mythology: Timeless Tales of Gods and Heroes*. New York: Mentor Books/The New American Library, Inc.

On Relationships and Emotions

Babiak, P., & Hare, R. (2006). *Snakes in Suits: When Psychopaths Go to Work*. New York: HarperCollins Publishers, Inc.

Chapman, G. (1992). *The Five Love Languages: How to Express Heartfelt Commitment to Your Mate*. Chicago: Northfield Publishing.

Goleman, D. (1995). *Emotional Intelligence: Why it can matter more than IQ*. New York: Bantam Books.

Gray, J. (1984). *What You Feel, You Can Heal: A Guide for Enriching Relationships*. Mill Valley, CA: Heart Publishing.

Gray, J. (1992). *Men are from Mars, Women are from Venus*. New York: HarperCollins Publishers, Inc.

Kiley, D. (1983). *The Peter Pan Syndrome: Men Who Have Never Grown Up*. New York: Dodd, Mead & Company, Inc.

Kiley, D. (1984). *The Wendy Dilemma: When Women Stop Mothering Their Men*. New York: Arbor House Publishing Company.

Lewis, M. (1992). *Shame: The Exposed Self*. New York: Free Press/MacMillan.

McKeon, R. (Ed.) (1947). The Poetics. *Introduction to Aristotle*. New York: Random House, Inc.

Siegel, E. (1981). *Self and World: An Explanation of Aesthetic Realism*. New York: Definition Press.

Steiner, C. (1974). *Scripts People Live: Transactional Analysis of Life Scripts*. New York: Bantam Books.

Stout, M. (2005). *The Sociopath Next Door: The Ruthless Versus the Rest of Us*. New York: Broadway Books/Random House.

Wisegeek.com. What is Catharsis? Retrieved from www.wisegeek.com/what-is-catharsis.htm (Accessed 8/13/2009)

REFERENCES

REFERENCES

Chapter 1: Why Apologize?

1. Covey, pp. 95–144; especially pp. 119–128.
2. Ibid., Appendix A: "If your center is Principles."
3. Coffman & Gonzalez-Molina, pp. 27, 99–124.

Chapter 2: Hidden Dynamics of Conversation

4. Carnegie, pp. 63–70; 71–79; 51–62; 89–93; 150–154; 80–88; 161–166; 167–174; 193–198; 191–236; 94–104; 116–126; 127–134.
5. Covey, pp. 188–203; especially pp. 190–198.
6. The Bolekian Focus Triangle is a previously unpublished conversation and conflict skills model originated by the author. It was co-developed between 2006 and 2008 in collaboration with Lee S. Johnsen, principal of Partners in Development, a leadership training and organizational development consulting firm located in Arlington Heights, Illinois.

Chapter 3: Apologies in the Big Picture

7. SoSuave.com, DeepBlue.
8. Covey, p. 197.
9. Gray (1992), p. 29.

Chapter 4: Apology Elements

10. Chapman and Thomas, p. 104.
11. Ibid., p. 106.

Chapter 5: Handling Feelings – Yours First

12. Gray (1984), pp. 137–183.
13. Kiley (1983).
14. Goleman, pp. 129–147.
15. Ibid., p. 43.
16. Ibid., p. 43.
17. Ibid., p. 283.
18. Covey., p. 18.

Chapter 6: Handling Her Feelings

19. Steiner, pp. 34–35, 60–64, 86–89, 119.
20. Ibid., pp. 175–178 (Dr. Karpman's victim-persecutor-rescuer triangle).
21. Gray (1992), pp. 36, 26, 35, 49.
22. Ibid., pp. 43, 133.
23. McKeon (Aristotle), p. 631.
24. Wisegeek.com.
25. Lewis, pp. 149–153, 186–187.
26. Siegel, p. 15.
27. Stout, pp. 46, 51.

Chapter 7: Typical Apologies: Part I

28. Kiley (1983), pp. 3–13.
29. Ibid., pp. 32–34.
30. SoSuave.com, Casanova.

Chapter 8: Typical Apologies: Part II

31. Hamilton, pp. 119, 160.
32. Ibid., pp. 154, 159–172.
33. Ibid., p. 163.
34. Ibid., p. 161.

ABOUT THE AUTHOR

Karen Field Bolek is a freelance editor and a creative thinker with a talent for developing original psychosocial models, including the Focus Triangle model for communication skills development shown in this book. She and her husband, James R. Bolek, have been married since 1980 and live in metropolitan Chicago. They have one daughter, Marisah Diana Bolek.

Karen holds a Master of Liberal Studies degree from Lake Forest College in Lake Forest, Illinois. Her first published work was a piano suite: *Inner Garden*, published by the Boston Music Company (B.M.Co. 14221) in 1992. This is her first book.

ABOUT THE RESEARCH

The Men's Apology Survey was developed by the author with guidance from Dr. Andrea Burleson-Rutter, an organizational psychologist with experience in developing surveys. The survey was conducted online via SurveyMonkey between September 2010 and January 2011. A total of 85 male and 85 female volunteers completed the survey. Overall, responses from men reflect a great deal of interest in the topics addressed in this book, and responses from women reveal relevant information about the desirability of various elements of an apology from their man.

To see the survey questions and a summary of the results, please visit: http://howtoapologizetoyourwoman.com.

Made in the USA
Coppell, TX
30 April 2022

77264515R00129